With my
to

BACK
WHEN

the story of
HISTORIC NEW MARKET
Maryland

J. Seng   1-29-06

JOSEPH F. SENG
EDITED BY EDGAR WILLIAM ROSSIG III

HERITAGE BOOKS
2005

HERITAGE BOOKS

AN IMPRINT OF HERITAGE BOOKS, INC.

Books, CDs, and more—Worldwide

For our listing of thousands of titles see our website
at
www.HeritageBooks.com

Published 2005 by
HERITAGE BOOKS, INC.
Publishing Division
65 East Main Street
Westminster, Maryland 21157-5026

International Standard Book Number: **0-7884-3599-X**

Blessed with pure water, good hygiene, pure air, and good crops, it is a pleasant place to live."

(From the General Directory of Frederick County of 1886, describing the Town of New Market, Maryland)

**Dedicated in Memory
of Our Beloved Son "Will"**

Photography

All photographs within this book not
specifically credited to others are images
made by the author between 2002 and 2004.

Format and Layout
By John J. Seng

Cover Design
By Mark Trinkaus

Acknowledgements

So many wonderful people have been helpful to me, both during my research and also while I was conducting personal interviews over the past two years. To begin with, I want to thank those who inspired me and encouraged me to take on this project. I also am very grateful to all who were so generous with their time, their information, and their old photographs. These good people are too numerous to acknowledge here individually, but their names appear throughout the chapters of this book.

Staff members and volunteers at the Historical Society of Frederick County were very helpful as were their counterparts at the Maryland Room of the Frederick County Library. As head of the New Market Historical Society, Edgar "Bud" Rossig played a key role in identifying sources and people who could be helpful and also by personally reviewing interim drafts from time to time and editing the final draft. I am very grateful to him. Others who assisted in this review included: Rita Mueller of New Market as well as my daughter Laura Marie Knutsen. My thanks also to Gene Rooney of New Market who graciously gave his written permission so that the title "Antiques Capital of Maryland"®, for which he owns the trademark, could be used in this book.

I especially want to express my gratitude to my son John J. Seng, President of Spectrum Science Communications in Washington, D.C., for his professional and technical assistance. Finally, I want to thank my wife Joyce for her encouragement and support throughout this project.

State of Maryland

Prologue

To begin our history of New Market, Maryland, we must journey back more than two centuries to a world far different from now. When New Market was founded in 1793, the French Revolution was going on in Europe. That year, under the so-called "Reign of Terror," both King Louis XVI of France and his wife Marie Antoinette were tried for treason and executed by guillotine.

Happier times meanwhile were being enjoyed elsewhere in Europe with the rise of perhaps the greatest classical musical composers of all time. Ludwig van Beethoven (1770-1827) of Germany is but one example. He composed important symphonies and also wrote music for operas and ballet. Austrian composers Franz Josef Haydn (1732-1809) and Wolfgang Amadeus Mozart (1756-1791) were other musical geniuses of the late eighteenth century when New Market was being settled.

In the New World, America's war for independence from Britain (1775-1782) had just ended. A United States constitution was drafted, debated, agreed upon, and then signed in 1789. Maryland was one of the original thirteen states signing the constitution. The same year, George Washington was inaugurated as the first U.S. president. Meanwhile, the dollar became the official U.S. currency, and there was an agreement that the national capital would be established on the banks of the Potomac River. In 1791, the Bill of Rights became law, amending the U.S. Constitution and guaranteeing the rights of all citizens. By 1800, the capital city of Washington was founded, and Baltimore was becoming a busy port.

The age of invention was in its infancy, but there were some notable developments during this same period. For example, the first working model of a mechanical telegraph was developed in Paris in 1787. Meanwhile, Scottish engineer James Watt's successful design of a steam engine, which was fully operable by 1788, led to extensive use of steam power in industry and transportation. William Murdoch invented gas lighting in Great Britain in 1792, and London streets featured such lights by 1807. The most significant U.S. invention of the time was Eli Whitney's development in 1793 of the cotton gin for separating cotton fiber from seeds. For the South in particular, this invention transformed its growing economy.

It also was a time of increasing immigration and settlement in the New World. By 1788, New Englanders had begun to settle in the Ohio Valley, and French Canadians settled in Illinois. By 1793, the Canadian city of Toronto was founded. Ten years later, the historic Louisiana Purchase from France greatly stimulated the settlement and growth of this young nation. It was in this time and context that what would become a unique town was founded in Frederick County, Maryland, forty miles west of Baltimore. This book tells the story of that very special town of **New Market**.

CONTENTS

Acknowledgements		vii
Prologue		ix
1.	Introduction	1
2.	The Founding Fathers of New Market	9
3.	The First Homes	23
4.	Utz Mercantile – Now the New Market General Store	53
5.	The Utz Hotel – Now Mealey's Restaurant	61
6.	The National Road	66
7.	The Coming of the Railroad	71
8.	Slavery in New Market	79
9.	The Civil War Days	87
10.	Local Churches	95
11.	Some Glimpses of Town Life in the 1800s and 1900s	103
12.	The New Market Grange	131
13.	"Antiques Capital of Maryland"®	139
14.	Local Government	153
15.	The Schools of New Market	163
16.	New Market Post Office	171
17.	Village Tea Room	179
18.	Annual Celebrations	181
19.	Volunteer Fire Company	201
20.	The Hahn Company	215
21.	Outlook for the Future	217
Appendix:	*Selected Bibliography*	225
	Personal Interviews	228
	About the Author	229

CHAPTER 1

Introduction

In the early 1700s, farmers of German heritage came to Maryland from Pennsylvania in search of good farmland, a favorable climate, and not-too-distant markets for their produce.[1] They came to an area known as the New Market Plains, situated in the Piedmont Plateau area, which extends east from the Catoctin Mountains. English, Scottish, and

Irish settlers soon followed, many of them coming from eastern Maryland. One of the latter was a Patrick Dulaney, who is credited with laying out "Fredericktown," now the City of Frederick, in 1745. Early settlers no doubt looked to Baltimore and nearby towns as potential markets for their produce. By 1760, the newly completed public road made it possible to transport more and more of these goods to Baltimore as well as to markets along the way.

Some of the early settlers were successful in obtaining large land grants from Lord Baltimore, the proprietor of Maryland in colonial times. One of the first tracts of land in the New Market District was via such a grant to John Dorsey, Jr., in

---

[1] T.J.C. Williams and Folger McKinsey, *History of Frederick County*, 1967 reprint of 1910 ed, Chicago, Vol. I, 1-2.

1743.[2] Other settlers there surveyed and established parcels or tracts of land with such colorful names as: "Darby's Delight," "Food Plenty," "Good Meadows," "Hall's Choice," "Help," "Hickory Plains," "Hunting Lot," "Peace and Plenty," "Pleasant Meddo," and "Rich Hills." These families - for example, the Halls, the Dorseys, and the Plummers - came to the New Market District in the late 1730s as its first pioneers. Men, women, and children cut logs from nearby woods and collected stones to build their homes, and they began to cultivate the land. The rich soil soon returned the favor by yielding bountiful harvests of wheat and corn.

Meanwhile, in 1748, Frederick County was established by an act of the Colonial Assembly (Acts of 1748, Chapter 15). Previously, the area had been part of Baltimore and Prince George's Counties. The new county included all of Western Maryland as well as what is now Montgomery County until the Constitutional Convention of 1776. Over 200 years later, Frederick County remains the largest county in Maryland with 664 square miles of land and six square miles of water surfaces. The county stretches from the Potomac River on the south to the Pennsylvania border on the north.

The early settlers of the New Market Plains and the other farmers of Frederick County made the most of its fertile soil and mild but humid climate. The farmers worked so successfully that, by 1790, Frederick County was the largest wheat-producing county in all of the thirteen states and one of the most productive agricultural counties in Maryland. The county's population at that time was 30,791. Moving produce and livestock to market was difficult at best in the late 1700s. Animals on hoof could not be driven more than seven or eight miles in one day. They also needed to be watered, rested, and sheltered for the night, as did those

[2] Ibid. 326.

farmhands who accompanied them. As a result, villages and towns emerged along the route to Baltimore. Eight miles east of Fredericktown would be the first stop, a place to be called **New Market**. Its location was at the crossroads of two historic Indian trails. One of these was a Seneca trail leading to mineral deposits in central Maryland. It forged the way for what is now Maryland Route 75. The other was the Great Indian Trail, which led westward forming a path for the present-day highways, U.S. Route 40 and Interstate 70.

The Road To New Market

By 1760, the development of the Public Road between Fredericktown and Baltimore greatly facilitated travel in the vicinity. Before that, the route had been no more than a trail. In the late 1700s, approaching New Market along the Public Road, however, had its ups and downs. Whether coming from the west or from the east, one would have to traverse a series of steep hills and dips that came to be known as "Whippoorwill Hollow" (to the west of town) and the "Seven Sisters" to the east. One can only marvel at the endurance of the early settlers, many on foot, traveling eight miles a day, uphill and downhill along the Frederick Road.

Eighteenth-Century Speed of Travel[3]

A person walking	4 - 5 MPH
Running fast	8 - 12 MPH
On horseback at a trot	5 - 10 MPH
On horseback at full speed	30 MPH, for short distances
Stagecoach	8 MPH
Wagon train on good road	up to 25 miles per day

Even in recent years, despite some minor downsizing of a few hills, the roller coaster nature of the road to New Market endures. I recall, when driving up and down these hills in the 1990s, how my young grandchildren exclaimed, "Grandpa, this is our favorite road!" Without even approaching the fifty mile-per-hour speed limit at that time, I could make them feel they were on a roller coaster, and we laughed about it.
    - JFS

(Note: Throughout this book, the initials "JFS" are used to identify the author's personal observations.)

In the early days of settlement, Main Street was dusty in good weather and very muddy on rainy days. For this reason, steppingstones were placed from one side of the road to the other so that people could cross the road more easily at its midpoint in town. Before dawn and after dusk, they must have had to be very cautious. It was not until 1885 that the town installed its first street lamps.

Facilities in Town

New Market served a very important role as a stopover point for weary travelers to stay, to unwind, and to take care of their immediate needs and those of their animals. Most

---

[3] Vera F. Rollo, *Your Maryland*, Maryland Historical Press, Lanham, Md., 3rd ed revised 1976, 196-203.

important were the hotels and taverns, as many as five to eight of them along the main street at various times. Four were said to be full-service hotels. Lodging for the night cost twenty-five cents. Likewise, there were inns where travelers could rest and refresh themselves. There also were about eight taverns where travelers could socialize or enjoy a glass of whiskey for merely a nickel. Small industries in town included a shoe factory, tanner, button-maker, wrought-iron nail shop, glass factory, saddle shop, and various blacksmiths. Merchants catered to the needs of residents and travelers alike, and wheelwrights built and repaired wagons.

Local carpenters/cabinetmakers such as Mortimer Falconer could make someone a table or other furniture or even build a log cabin home. Logs were cut from wonderful chestnut trees so plentiful in the area in those days - and now almost extinct. Falconer's business continued in his family for generations. Another local carpenter, Arthur Tansey, offered this special: For two dollars, he would make a cradle or a coffin, depending on whether one was entering or leaving this world.

Meanwhile, various mills began to appear along streams in the vicinity of New Market. For example, Anthony Poultney built a sawmill just a mile to the south in Monrovia, and John Ijams started a gristmill a few miles to the west in what became the village of Ijamsville (pronounced "Iyamsville"). Evern Dorsey built a mill in New London, a few miles north of New Market, in 1804. Also to the north, other mills began operating in the Linganore vicinity. In 1805, a Scotsman named Robinson built a woolen mill along Bush Creek in Monrovia. Most important, however, were the flourmills that were needed to process all the wheat that was being grown by local farmers. The flour produced became widely known for its quality, and the mills flourished until about 1870.

New Market had a parking problem in its earliest years, just as it does currently. To begin with, the high-wheeled Conestoga wagons had to be parked off-street in open fields. Pens had to be provided for farm animals being driven by herdsmen on their way to market. The town played a very important role in providing both the facilities and the services needed by travelers to the east and to the west, especially during the nineteenth century.

What New Market lacked most in its earliest years was a grocery. Nor was there a place to buy articles of clothing or building materials. Pioneers such as Nicholas Hall and, later, Ed Adams took it upon themselves to circulate through town taking orders for food or other necessities before making a day's shopping trip to Fredericktown and back, for a slight fee. Newspapers were circulated to townspeople and farmers in the same manner. Small groceries eventually arrived in New Market, operating out of homes, inns, or hotels at various times. Reportedly in 1842, one of these small groceries charged twenty-five cents for a pound of butter and twelve cents for a dozen eggs. A pound of coffee sold for fourteen cents. But groceries never remained permanently. Even at the present time, there is no grocery, hardware store, or clothing establishment in town.

A Special Place?

It was not until March 1878 that the Town of New Market was incorporated. At the time, the town had a population of 402. Surprisingly, an estimate in 1969 showed no significant increase, and the U.S Census of 2000 counted only 427 persons there in 159 households. New Market has survived for 212 years even though it may be one of the smallest towns in the United States.[4] In 1975, it was registered as an **Historic District** in the U.S. Department of the Interior's National Register. Perhaps there is something special about this place.

Frederick County's early history also is rich in names. Francis Scott Key, who wrote "The Star Spangled Banner," was born there as was Dr. Samuel Hansen, a Revolutionary War surgeon. Likewise, Governor Thomas Johnson, Maryland's first governor, and Supreme Court Chief Justice Roger Brooke Taney were Frederick County natives. (Taney is known for his controversial decision in the Dred Scott Case of 1857 in which the Court ruled that the Congress could not bar slavery in the U.S. territories.)

All of the above figures in history are buried in the City of Frederick.

[4] *New Market Region Plan* (staff draft) Frederick Conty Division of Planning, November 2003, 46.

Imprint of New Market Justice of the Peace Seal, c. 1800. According to local historian Edgar W. Rossig, III, there was a small jail or holding cell in the town. Prisoners could be held there until they could be transferred to Fredericktown for a bond hearing.

CHAPTER 2

The Founding Fathers
Of New Market

Nicholas Hall

Nicholas Hall was born in about 1756, twenty years before America's Declaration of Independence.[5] He was of English stock and had traveled to Frederick County to manage properties owned by his uncle, William Hall of Elkridge, Maryland, which was then the second leading tobacco port in the state. Elkridge is on the Patapsco River, southwest of Baltimore. Hall's grandfather, Henry Hall, had served in the Maryland Legislature for many years. He was a member when the first General Assembly met in 1777 and elected Maryland's first governor, Thomas Johnson.

Nicholas Hall, however, was more interested in land development than in politics. He and his brother William Hall, Jr., were property owners as early as 1781, according to Frederick County land records. Nicholas bought out William and accumulated several properties in the county, including 2,000 acres in the New Market area. At this time, he was still a very young man, in his twenties, but anxious to make his mark in this new land.

Susan Wilson knows something about this eighteenth-century entrepreneur. She is a seventh-generation descendant of Nicholas Hall and Anne Griffith, whom he married in 1779.

[5] Susan Wilson, *New Market and its Relationship With the World at Large*, Timeline, Wilson Information Services, 1997.

Susan still resides in the family farm home on Baldwin Road, with her husband Howard Wilson and son Nathaniel. Hall built the original wood part of the structure on a hill in 1780, Sue relates, "but he later had to move it down from the hill, where water could be found." The brick portion of the house was added in the early 1800s.

Sue Wilson and her brother Nicholas Wood (left) are the only offspring of Charles W. Wood, now deceased, and his widow Mary Wood, who resides in a Frederick nursing home. Charles Wood operated a bookstore for many years in New Market, across from the former post office, which is now the Town Hall. Nick and his wife Susan Wood live in their own home on the back part of the family farm property.

Unfortunately, Hall's descendants have no idea what he looked like, whether he was tall or short, whether he was blonde, red-haired, or dark. There was no photography in those times. Susan tells how itinerant artists would stay with a family for a time while painting family portraits. When finished, they would collect their pay and then move on to another customer's home. No such portrait of Nicholas has been found, however. What we do know about him and his wife, Anne Griffith Hall, is that they were a young couple, like many today, just starting out, wanting to have a nice place to live and to raise a family of their own. By today's standards, they might be considered over-achievers in that they had six children born to them in only eight years. On the other hand, the survival rate for children was not what it is today. (The Halls suffered the loss of two of their young boys.):

- Elizabeth, born in 1780, married John Pitts, a famous Methodist minister. (The couple resided in the home built by her father.)
- Henry, born in 1782, died in 1788 at the age of six.
- Nicholas, Jr., was born in 1784.
- John was born in 1785 and died in 1788 at the age of three, within two months of his brother Henry's death.
- Ann was born in 1787 and Eleanor in 1788.[6]

According to Nick Wood, the Hall Family made much of their income from selling merchandise from a store in their backyard. The small white building with its tin roof is still there. Nick points out that there once was a cannon placed in front of the store. When the Halls received a shipment of goods, they would fire the cannon to let people know that their orders could be filled. Nick describes it as a general merchandise store selling many things, such as cloth, flour, and foodstuffs. Later, this same building served as the "overseer's house." (See Chapter 8, "Slavery in New Market.")

It was in 1787 that Hall embarked on his first attempt to set out a town and to sell lots out of the land grant that he had received. The site he chose was on either side of the public road.

---

[6] Ibid.

Laid out for a TOWN,
TO BE CALLED
NEWMARKET.

AND now for SALE, on the public Road, from Frederick-Town to Baltimore, about nine miles from Frederick; one hundred and seventeen Lots, and a number more to be laid off if neceſſary.

Two principal Streets in this Town, one 66 feet, the other fifty feet wide, three others 33 feet wide, and the Alleys 16 1-2 feet wide.

The Lots are 66 feet front, 165 feet back, and one fifth of the Lots have the advantage of bounding on two Streets, or an Alley, and all confined on a Street or Alley; there is a reſerve of ground for a Market-Houſe, and a Church.

The Situation of this place is exceedingly pleaſant and remarkable healthy. I think it unneceſſary to ſay any thing with regard to the ſoil, as the place is well known. The Lots are Sold by the Subſcriber, living near the Premiſes. Lots bounding on the main public Street, will be Sold for THREE POUNDS Current money each. The Lots back at FORTY SHILLINGS each; all ſubject to an annual Ground-Rent of Five Shillings current money, to commence from the firſt day of May 1788.

Any Purchaſer not complying with the terms abovementioned, doth forfeit their Lot to the Proprietor, or his Heirs or Aſſigns, and their Leaſe to be of non-effect; the Lots to be Conveyed by Leaſe for 99 years and renewable fore ver.

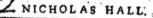 NICHOLAS HALL.

Hall's plan provided for six streets. Two of them would be 66 feet wide, one 50 feet wide, and three 33 feet in width. Lots were to be large, 66 by 165 feet each. Two of them would be reserved respectively for a market house and a church, as shown in this copy of Hall's own advertisement, "Laid out for a Town to be called New Market." A unique term of the sale was the provision for ground rent to be paid by the buyer or subsequent buyers as specified in a 99-year lease, renewable forever. [The Maryland state legislature outlawed such ground rent in 1820.] Hall's advertisement appeared in a Frederick County newspaper, **The Maryland Chronicle**, on 2 May 1787, just one year after that newspaper was started.

It was a very good effort by this then thirty-one-year-old pioneer, but no lots were sold. Hall and his wife must have been very disappointed. He had to step back and reconsider his approach, but he was not disillusioned. Hall would not give up. He would persevere in his efforts. In the next few years, he was to form an alliance with another local entrepreneur. There would be a New Market, Maryland.

Hall being of English heritage might have had something to do with the choice of names for his new town. According to a family legend, "New Market" was named after New Market, sometimes spelled "Newmarket," England, a town known for raising horses. It is thirty miles north of London and just east of Cambridge.   - JFS

The First Plummers

Thomas Plummer (the first of many by that name) came to Maryland from England in 1667.[7][8]   He settled in Anne Arundel County, acquired a considerable amount of land there, and married Elizabeth Stockett. The couple had five children. Their oldest, Thomas (#2), was born in about 1670

[7] Elise Greenup Jourdan, *Early Families of Southern Maryland: The Plummer Family,* Vol. II, Family Line Publications, Westminster, Md., 1993, 1-17.

[8] Herbert F. Smith, *The Plummer Ancestry of Herbert F. Smith,* indexed and produced by Robert S. Smith, Historical Society of Frederick County, 1995.

and later settled in what was then Prince George's County, where he too accumulated land. He married Elizabeth Smith, and their marriage was a very fruitful one. (Very large families were not unusual among early Maryland pioneers. Children were needed to help with chores and to work the land, as they grew old enough.) The Plummers had a dozen youngsters. Their ten sons included Thomas (#3), Samuel, George, James, John, Jerome, Philemon, Micajah, Yate, and Abiezer. Their two daughters were named Priscilla and Phoebe.

Four of the sons were destined to play significant roles in the development of what is now Frederick County, Maryland. The growth began with a series of land surveys from 1739 to 1743.[9]

- Philemon Plummer had a land survey made on 13 September 1739 for a fifty-acre parcel of land called "Debutt's Delight." It was located in the forks of a branch to the south of Linganore Creek, close to the current-day Spring Ridge development and nearby filtration plant. (This land subsequently became part of "Hammond's Request" during an 1812 survey.) In 1744, Philemon died. His widow Elizabeth was left with their nine children, only one of whom, John, was an adult.
- Samuel Plummer's fifty-acre survey was on the west side of Bennett Creek, to the east of Sugar Loaf Mountain in the vicinity of present-day community of Thurston. More significant to the development of New Market, however, were the four surveys he filed on 28 June 1743. They were "Rich Hills," just west of what is

[9] J. Thomas Scharf, A.M., *History of Western Maryland*, Regional Publishing Co., Baltimore, 1968 Reprint of 1882 ed., 228-236.

now Crickenberger Road; "Hunting Lot," (variously called "Hunting Lott" or "Hunting Loot") just north of today's New Market; "Pleasant Meddo," part of present-day Monrovia in the forks of Bush Creek; and, just to the east, "Food Plenty."

- Micajah Plummer likewise had a fifty-acre survey done for himself on 7 April 1743. Called "Plummer's Delight," it was located on a small branch running into Bush Creek, west of the current-day New Market-Monrovia area, which also is along Bush Creek. The fifty acres are in the area of today's Thurston and Slate Quarry Roads on the east side of Sugarloaf Mountain.

- Thomas Plummer (son of Thomas and Elizabeth) began to acquire land in Frederick County in 1744. His properties were further north on Bush Creek and also along a branch of Bennett Creek (in southern Frederick County).

Samuel Plummer Family

Samuel Plummer was born in Prince George's County, Maryland on 9 February 1701. He was named the sole beneficiary in the estate of Richard Rose of that county in June 1717. As the result of this good fortune, Plummer added "Rose's Purchase" to his homestead there, which also included his own plantation called "Upper Getting." He became known as Samuel Plummer of Prince George's County. Additionally, Samuel owned almost 2,000 acres in the New Market/Monrovia area of today. He married Sarah Miles in 1724, and, just like his own parents had done, they had twelve children. In this case, there were four sons and eight daughters:

- Thomas, who married Eleanor Walker Poultney, the

widow of John Poultney.

- Joseph, who married Sarah Sollers. They had ten children and lived in his father's "Pleasant Meddo" section (now Monrovia). When his father died in 1754, Joseph increased the land there to 412 acres. In 1764, he further enlarged it to 1,777 acres and changed its name to "Land of Promise."
- Samuel, Jr., who married Mary Tucker and inherited the fifty-acre "Plummer's Delight," which was expanded in 1760.
- Abraham, who married Sarah Ward and inherited "Hickory Plains," which was not laid out until 1750.
- Ruth, who married Richard Holland, owner of Bush Creek Mountain.
- Cassandra, who married William Ballenger, the son of pioneer Henry Ballenger.
- Sarah, who married Mahlon Janney.
- Rachel, who married John Harris.
- Elizabeth, who married Moses Harris.
- Anna, who married Joseph Talbert.
- Suzanna, who married Anthony Poultney. (He is known for having established a sawmill in Monrovia in 1790.)
- Ursula, who never married.

In 1747, the Samuel Plummer Family donated four acres of land in the Bush Creek area to the Society of Friends, i.e. Quakers. It was there that this group built its log meeting house, which was the site of well-attended regular meetings, weddings, and other social events. (Minutes of these meetings comprised a valuable source of information for this book.)

Family of Thomas Plummer

Thomas Plummer, the son of Samuel and Sarah, was born in 1726. In 1761, Thomas married Eleanor Poultney, who came to be called Ellen. They had four children: Isaac, Jesse, Ruth, and William, who, along with Nicholas Hall, established the Town of New Market. When Thomas died in 1784, he left this will:[10]

> *Will dtd.20th day 6th month 1777, in health. To wife Ellen: plantation with liberty to take timber for improvements for life; if she remarries, her thirds and the rest to son Isaac; also to Ellen: one riding creature, 2 cows, and one-third personal estate. To son Isaac: tract Saplin Hill Resurveyed. To sons Jesse and William: tract Hunting Lott, Jesse to have the improved part; if they fail, land to dau. Ruth; also to Ruth: 50 (pounds). Executor to give wife working tools with wagon, then to Isaac. Friend and brother-in-law William Ballinger executor. /s/ Wit: Samuel Waters, William Morsell, Robert Hunt. Proved 11 Nov. 1784. (121-123)*

Thus it was that William Plummer would come into possession of land in the vicinity of present-day New Market, possibly buying out his brother Jesse's share of Hunting Lott.

William Plummer

Thomas Plummer's son William was born on 27 November 1770 and died 2 June 1856. It is thought that he may have been a surveyor. On 1 November 1792, William married Rachel Morsell, daughter of William and Mary Morsell, at a

---

[10] Register of Wills for Frederick County, Maryland (1783-1794), Thomas Plummer, Liber GM-2-121.

Bush Creek Meeting of the local Quakers.   Most of the
Plummers were active Quaker members.

Various sources of information about the Plummer Family
indicate that there were several William Plummers and their
wives. For example, a William Plummer married Margaret
Jones in 1779.   Another married Linney Ann Hoggins in
1791, and still another married Rachel Hobbs in 1795 – all
according to a Genealogical Index to Frederick County,
Maryland.[11]   The same Genealogical Index identifies
William Plummer, the son of Thomas, as marrying Rachel
Morsell in 1792. It is the belief of this writer that this is the
William Plummer of interest here. Evidence to support this
view is contained in the publication *Early Families of
Southern Maryland*, which states:[12]

> *122-4 William Plummer, b. 27 Nov 1770; m. 1 Nov
> 1792 Bush Creek Meeting to Rachel Morsell; d/o
> William and Mary Morsell; 1 June 1793 he laid out
> part of New Market, MD [co-founder]; Nicholas Hall
> was also selling land of this town, which was part of
> Dorsey's Partnership; children, probably not in
> order of birth:*
>
> *1224-1 Thomas Morsell Plummer; m. Mary West*
> *1224-2 William W. Plummer*
> *1224-3 Rachel Plummer*
> *1224-4 Rebekah Plummer*
> *1224-5 Mary, m. Abraham Johns*
> *1224-6 Elizabeth Plummer; unmarried*
> *1224-7 Ellen Plummer*
> *1224-8 Jesse, m. Mary G. Russell*

A second source for the November 1792 wedding of William

[11] John Stanwood Martin, *Genealogical Index to Frederick Country, Maryland*, Vol III,
Conlin's Copy Center, Malvern, Pa., 1992.
[12] *Early Families of Southern Maryland - The Plummer Family*, Vol. II, 1993, 1-17.

Plummer to Rachel Morsell is in the Quaker Records of Northern Maryland, Pipe Creek Monthly Meeting, which identifies this William as being the son of Thomas Plummer and Ellen his wife.[13] William's mother Ellen and his siblings Isaac, Jesse, and Ruth all were listed as among the many witnesses at this wedding. William Plummer's birth date is recorded as the "27th day, 11th month, 1770."

The William Plummers lived on a farm, just north and west of the town site that later was laid out by Nicholas Hall. Plummer offered some lots for sale on the south section of his farm, but none was sold. He did build the first house in what is now New Market. It was a two-story log cabin that has been improved and enlarged over the years and still stands at 51 Main Street.

William Plummer had much in common with Hall. Both were ambitious young men. Each man was married and starting to raise a family. Both had land that they wanted to develop for selling lots. Much like their counterparts of today, they wanted homes, and they wanted a town and all the services it could provide for themselves, for their families, and for their fellow settlers.

Nicholas Hall - William Plummer Ventures

Both Hall and Plummer had failed in their first attempts to sell lots. Perhaps it was that each individually lacked experience, resources, or skills to be successful in real estate. In 1787, Hall had attempted to develop plans for a town along the Public Road but failed. Plummer owned the adjacent land, but the two could not agree on the road alignment or layout of lots.

[13] Henry C. Peden, Jr., M.A. *Quaker Records of Northern Maryland, Births, Deaths, Marriages and Abstracts from the Minutes of Monthly Meetings, 1716-1800*, Pipe Creek Monthly Meeting, 258-259, 273-279, Family Line Publications, Westminster, Md., 1993.

Some distance to the rear of the ancestral home of Nicholas Hall is the family cemetery where Nicholas Hall is buried along with his immediate family members. Nick Wood led the way through tall grass that all but hid most of the markers from view. One stone stood above all the rest, identifying the grave of New Market founder Nicholas Hall, with his name and the date of his death, 1821.

On 1 August 1792, Plummer laid out thirty-six lots on land (i.e., Hunting Lott) that he and his brother Jesse had inherited from their father Thomas, as described previously. This section of lots subsequently came to be known as "Plummer's Part of New Market." William built homes there for two of his aunts, Ursula and Ruth Plummer, and Jesse came to live there as well.

Only seven months later, on 29 January 1793, Hall laid out 134 lots of his own just to the east of Plummer's section on land known as Dorsey's Partnership. It is considered that the Town of New Market originated when Hall advertised and sold his first nineteen lots on 1 June 1793.[14] The town layout featured a single main street, one-half mile in length, along the Public Road, with a grid of large lots on either side of it. Two lesser roads paralleled Main Street, one to the north and one to the south, and numerous small alleys further subdivided the lots.

The combined ventures by Hall and Plummer in 1793 were remarkably successful. They continued to sell many additional lots in the years that followed. Roadwork begun in 1805 on the Baltimore-Fredericktown Turnpike, which would follow the Public Road directly through New Market, secured the continuing success of their ventures.

Hall died in 1821 and Plummer in 1856. Copies of their last wills and testaments are on file at the Frederick County Courthouse.[15]

---

[14] J. Thomas Scharf, A.M. *History of Western Maryland*, Regional Publishing Co. Baltimore, 1968 Reprint of 1882 ed., 607-608.

[15] Register of Wills for Frederick County, Maryland (1783-1794), Nicholas Hall, Liber HS-2-422, 9 January 1821; William Plummer, Liber GH-1-140, 2 June 1856.

Street Map From 1873 Titus Atlas.

CHAPTER 3

The First Homes

The Fehr House

As mentioned previously, William Plummer built his two-story cabin before other homes were constructed in New Market, but it was just outside the town limits of the 1793 town plan, at what is now 51 W. Main Street. Scharf's **History of Western Maryland**[16] reveals that Thomas Plummer transferred this property, known as Lot 4, to his son, William Plummer, on 20 June 1777. William built his house there, and he and his descendants occupied it for more than a century.

William's daughter Rachel sold the Plummer farm in 1880 but retained the family home where she continued to reside.

The Historical Society of Frederick County maintains a file of such historic properties in the county, including eighteen landmark structures in or near the Town of New Market. Each bears an individually numbered landmark plaque on the front of the building, usually near the front door. Since 1975, the Historical Society has maintained a file of information, with the corresponding plaque number, for each of these historic properties. The Fehr House was designated Landmark Plaque Number 114.

[16] See Note 14.

The Plummer home became known as the Fehr House after Pat Vankirk Fehr and Cynthia S. Fehr bought it in January 1965 and operated an antique shop there for a number of years. The Fehrs bought this historic property from Stoll Kemp and his wife Katherine. Kemp became the very first antique dealer in New Market. (See Chapter 13, "Antiques Capital of Maryland.®") The Fehrs sold the property to Larry and Margie Pipes in 1988, and, for a time, they also kept an antique shop there.

Over the years, several artifacts have been found in the home, including a circa-1800 bone-handled fork; a hand-forged nail; a hand-split oak lathing strip; and a hand-tapered beam peg.

The Fehr House features the original glass windows, moldings, random-width oak floors, and staircase, and is considered a good example of the colonial period. Originally, the house had a fireplace in each room, only three of which remain since central heating was installed. The style of house was called an "Adam House" or "Adam/Farrell House" in that it had two rooms up and two rooms down with one staircase going up the wall on the right side of the house. (The home of New Market's co-founder, Nicholas Hall, features the same type of colonial staircase.)

The left (west) side of the house, a log structure, was built first, and the right (east) side, constructed of wood, was added after 1800. Another addition subsequently was constructed in the back of the house, with one room on each floor. The property also includes its original well, an outhouse, chicken coop, workshop, and now a carriage house.

Home of Ursula Plummer

Recent Photo at the Back of Ursula's Log House and its Original Well, Now Capped with Concrete.

A log house that William Plummer built in 1798 for his aunt, Ursula Plummer (1742-1816), also still stands at 37 W. Main Street.[17] [18] Ursula, the daughter of Samuel and Sarah Plummer, was a spinster, (as noted in Chapter 1). She paid seventy-five pounds for the property, which was known as Lot #1 in Plummer's Part of "New Market Plains." Smaller than most lots in town, it measured 24 by 165 feet. Ursula's sister, Ruth, bought two lots in New Market at the same time.

Ursula's log house, which has one large room at the ground level as well as a bedroom above, often goes unnoticed. Currently, there is no sign to call it to one's attention. Furthermore, it is mostly hidden by subsequent additions to the front of it. In fact, the home as one sees it today consists of eighteenth-, nineteenth-, and twentieth-century sections, each typifying the architecture of the time. The final segment, strangely, was but a five-foot addition to the front of the house at the turn of the century (i.e., circa 1900).

---

[17] John Stanwood Martin, *Genealogical Index to Frederick County, Maryland*, Vol. III, Conlin's Copy Center, Malvern, Pa., 1992.

[18] Elise Greenup Jourdan, *Early Families of Southern Maryland: The Plummer Family*, Vol I., Family Line Publications, Westminster, Md., 1993, 8.

The home is an unusual but significant structure. It is listed in the National Historic Register. How strange, then, it is to learn that it was auctioned off for a modest bid of $19,600 in 1977. It seems all the more remarkable that William and Colleen Shook bought the property at a sidewalk auction in New Market. They had hoped to fix up the home and use it as an antique shop. In fact, they hired Edgar Rossig, Jr., of New Market to refurbish the building with special attention to the original log portion. He had been doing other restoration work in town.

Rossig, for example, replaced chinking that had disintegrated between many of the chestnut logs. In the process of uncovering and exposing these logs, he discovered that the outside of the logs had been whitewashed, as was the custom in colonial times. Once the log portion of the house was restored, work continued over a two and one-half-year period to restore the later sections of the home. During this process, Rossig uncovered a fireplace in the living room and another in a bedroom of the 1830 section of the house.

Just to the rear of Ursula's log home one can see the cap over the original town well. Further back there is a very old shed and beyond that a "garage" possibly used to shelter carriages at one time.

This small home is a delight to see. There certainly is more to it than one might guess just viewing it from the street. The rooms are charming, the staircases very narrow, some of the ceilings extremely low, and the bathroom as tiny as could be. It would seem to be a fine place for an antique shop or even a small bed and breakfast perhaps. Unfortunately for the Shooks, the town authorities ultimately would not permit them to operate a business there because the lot size was too small. Colleen and her husband Bill were disappointed but undaunted. They rented out Ursula's Home and bought another New Market property, the "1812 House," on the other side of the street. It was there that they finally established their own antique shop. That building, at 48 West Main Street, is among the "Landmark Properties" described later in this chapter.

The Smith Tavern

The first structure built within the town limits was the "Smith Tavern" at 17 East Main Street. It is on the east end of town at the northwest corner of Federal Street and Main. It was built in 1793 by George Smith, as a residence with a tavern on the lower level.[19] The Smith Tavern was a popular place for travelers to stay, refresh themselves, eat, drink, and socialize. It also was important because of its strategic location across the road from a large well, which has since been rebuilt but still exists in the same location.

---

[19] T.J.C. Williams and Folger McKinsey, *History of Frederick Country, Maryland*, 1967 reprint of 1910 ed., 326.

Other than Main Street, the "Road to Monrovia" (now comprised of Eighth Alley and Prospect Alley) was the only other main road in New Market. It connected the town with Monrovia just to the south but also extended all the way to Libertytown, seven miles to the north. (This road served as Maryland Route 75 for many years until its realignment in connection with changes to Route 40 and the development of Interstate 70 bypassing New Market.) In early times, Route 75 crossed over a number of private farm properties between New Market and Libertytown. It is said that the farmers wanted to be paid for this public use of their land, and this may be the reason that this route failed.

The original Smith cabin has been enlarged over the years, but its chestnut logs are still intact and visible in several rooms and in the attic. Also surviving are the original plastered walls, reinforced with horse hair, some of the original doors and hinges, fluted wood trim, and antique windows with their typically irregular glass panes. Large corncobs were used for insulating the walls.

Jim Higgs and his wife Bonnie have owned the Smith Tavern property since 1989. It is their home and their antique business as well, thus the current name, "Smith Tavern Antiques." Jim notes that their place is open most days of the week, when they are not away. The couple travels to London every year to buy antiques to sell in their New Market shop. Jim says that many of their customers come from Washington, D.C.

His house is more than 200 years old, and Jim loves to tell about it. For example, he points out that hiding shoes in the attic rafters was a custom of the late 1700s and early 1800s. One would hide a shoe in the attic to ward off evil spirits.

Sometimes people also would hide a baby's shoe in the belief that this would protect the home from fire. While doing some repairs, Jim found such a shoe between the attic joists.

George Smith died in 1826 and, according to Higgs, "left a bunch of children." Smith had changed his will more than once, and his heirs were in and out of the will at various times. The home reportedly was bought and sold several times in the 1830s and 1840s for sums ranging from $300 to $400. From 1855 to 1885, it was a Methodist parsonage. A square addition was added to the rear of the building during that period.

According to Jim, there were old wagon ruts, with a hump in the middle behind his place years ago. He points out, "They used to shoe horses in back, near the barn. That's where the blacksmith worked." Higgs says the area basically was untouched for many years before he bought the place. The wagon ruts long since have been filled in with stone.

1-cent reward for return of indentured servant.

$10 reward for return of horse or donkey.

Smith Tavern Advertisement in a Fredericktown Newspaper, *The Federal Gazette*, on 20 April 1797.

Other Landmark Properties in or Near New Market

(Properties are described successively as one proceeds from east to west through New Market.)

The Brinkley Farm – Landmark Plaque Number 122: The historic brick farmhouse sits on thirty-five acres of land in the northeast section of town at 5519 Old New Market Road. The property originally comprised some 127 acres and was a dairy farm, which provided milk to the early residents of New Market. The two-story brick house was built in 1813, but parts of it may be even older. It had a slate roof and several chimneys.

Dr. George Ross Brinkley, Jr., and his wife Jean Tonkin Brinkley bought the house and farm from previous owners by the name of Burgess in about 1958. Mrs. Brinkley recalls some of the features of the farmhouse as they found it back then:

- The brick is original but has been painted. Over the years, the bricks have become soft. Mrs. Brinkley recalls how her husband once leaned against one of the chimneys while he was talking to an architect, and his hand went right through the chimney.
- When the house was built, the beams were marked with Roman numerals, indicating where they were to go. The numerals are still visible. The Brinkleys also found evidence of corncobs that had been used to insulate the walls.
- The house had extremely steep stairways. For example, steps went from the front door straight up to the

bedrooms above. When the Brinkleys restored the home in 1959, they finally found a way to redesign the staircase with a landing between two shorter flights of stairs that were not so steep.

- Plumbing included a single cold-water tap. There also was a hand-dug well out back. It was only thirty-six feet deep but never went dry. Water was needed to cool the nearby milk house.

When the Brinkleys bought the place in 1958, they were amazed to find that the house harbored a very strange place - an empty room that had been sealed off from the rest of the house. It had no means of access and no closets or other signs of how it had been used, if at all. Also peculiar was the fact that wide oak planks, with tongue-and-groove joints, were used to floor the attic while less permanent pine planks were used downstairs in the living quarters. When the latter rotted out, the heavy oak planks were laboriously carried down to replace the old pine.

There was an outhouse, of course, as well as a small barn out back. The barn was unusually tall for its size. It originally featured two stories, the lower story being used for milking cows and the upper part of the barn for storing hay. Mrs. Brinkley explained that her family converted the barn to one story because the upper floor could not support the weight of baled hay. In the old days, before farmers baled their hay, they just tossed the hay into the upper barn, and the weight of the loose hay was much less than stacks of baled hay would be.

Dr. and Mrs. Brinkley raised four children on this farm. "It was a wonderful place to raise children," Jean recalls, adding, "I thoroughly enjoyed it." Their son is Maryland State

Senator David Brinkley. Their daughter Susan, following in her father's footsteps, became a doctor. Another daughter, Norma has a health-related job in government, and Elizabeth married a local builder, Mike Sponseller.

The Brinkleys also raised ponies for hunting. The parents and all four children rode and would go fox hunting together. Jean treasures a photograph of all six family members mounted on horseback in front of the old farmhouse. They kept twenty-seven hounds in the back barn, for fox hunting purposes. "They got loose one day," Jean remembers, "and went through town chasing a dog. The town folks (in New Market) screamed and hollered and rushed to bring their kids in." She can laugh about it now. It happened in about 1960.

After her husband passed away, Jean Brinkley left the family farm and now lives a few miles away on fifteen acres of land where she still keeps horses. She gave the old farm to her children, who subsequently sold it. In 1999, the Town of New Market annexed the property. Currently, there are plans for a housing development to be built there by D.R. Horton, a Texas-based firm. The development, called "Brinkley Manor," is to have eighty-six single-family homes and twenty-three townhouses, with construction to beginning in 2004. An additional development, "The Orchard at New Market," is at the east edge of town, on forty-four acres of land near the intersection of Routes 144 and 75. (See Chapter 14.)

"The Nathan House" at 1 E. Main St. – Landmark Plaque Number 101: A log and frame structure was built at this site in about 1840 on a lot purchased by George Morrison in the mid-1790s. The place served as a residence and a grocery for a time. The original building and store subsequently burned down, and the current brick home was built in 1913. During the 1940s, a local physician, Dr. Ernest Roop, had his office and residence there. (See Chapter 11, "Some Glimpses of Local Life in the 1800s and 1900s"). The owner was listed as M. J. Warfield at the time of application for landmark status. Subsequent owners have included Mr. and Mrs. Arthur Caulfield and, currently, Mr. and Mrs. Will Rosenauer.

The Methodist Protestant Church, built in 1831, and its cemetery adjoined the property at 1 E. Main St. prior to the period that Dr. Roop lived there. (Refer to Chapter 10, "Local Churches").

Residence at 1 S. Federal St. – Landmark Plaque Number 57: The Historical Society's Landmark File states that this residence, originally a one and one-half-story log farmhouse, was built in either 1790 or 1830. In about 1840, a wing was added and the roof was raised to make it a full two-story home. Edgar Rossig, Jr., a local resident who performed

other restoration work in New Market, restored this home in 1974. Margaret P. MacNair owned the property at that time. Someone by the name of Michon was listed as the owner since 1985, and Margaret P. MacNair was the name on the application for a landmark plaque. Its current owners, Leonard Curry and Cyndie Koe, bought the property after a foreclosure in 2001 and have continued restoration.

The original town well, near 1 S. Federal Street, remains much as it was 200 years ago.

New Market United Methodist Church – Landmark Plaque Number 51: This historic church is located a block off the Main Street on North Alley at Route 874.

Buildings at 1-3 W. Main St. – Landmark Plaque Number 225: These buildings were constructed of brick and stone in about 1837. They have been described as good examples of early townhouses during that period. The one at the Number 3 address includes ten rooms and was a button factory in its earliest years. A porch and dining room were added later. The other building had a shop and apartment

First New Market Gas Pump at 1 W. Main Street in 1930. Stier Family Photo Courtesy of Bud Rossig.

with six rooms, where Mrs. Frances I. Mealey, original owner of Mealey's Restaurant, lived. (See Chapter 5, "The Utz Hotel – Now Mealey's Restaurant.") There also was a circa-1847 stable on the property.

Former National Hotel at 5 W. Main St. – Landmark Plaque Number 011: This building, reportedly built during the last quarter of the eighteenth century, has a long and colorful history. In its earliest years, it served as an inn - an important stopover place for travelers passing through New

Market. It has been said that lodgers on the top floors could not exit the inn without passing through the innkeeper's bedroom, thus insuring that no one left without paying his bill. The building was entered in the National Register in December 1975.

This historic structure has been used as a hotel, stage office, tavern, post office, library, general store, and Scottish imports shop. Despite all the changes in its use over the past two centuries, the building looks much as it did in historic pictures of years ago with its double chimneys, period shutters, and Flemish Bond brick masonry. The hotel was built in four stages, starting in about 1795. There were c.1809 additions to the front and to the east side. A courtyard and living room above the courtyard were not added until the mid-1900s.

Hamilton Stier and his descendants owned this property during his four terms as New Market Postmaster (at various times between 1841 and 1870) and well beyond that. One of his descendants visited New Market as recently as 2004 and stayed at the Strawberry Inn while in town.

Before entering the building, one may notice the small brick-and-stone platform once used by carriage passengers and drivers arriving at the hotel to dismount. Originally situated at the front door, the platform was moved alongside the driveway by more recent owners. Local legends have it that this platform may have been used for the auction of slaves in the early to mid-1800s.

"The National Hotel" sign now hanging in the front hall is original, dating back to 1840 and testifying to the building's use as such to that date or before then. Amazingly, the original lock and key are still on the front door. Likewise, the stair railing and newel posts are original features.

The Hotel originally offered nine bedrooms and a ballroom, which later was converted to a master bedroom. The old tavern room is just to the right as one enters the building, with the "whiskey room" (keeping room) just off its main room. Whiskey kegs once were rolled up into this room from the cellar, where they were stored, through a trap door. The trap door still exists and can be seen by lifting the carpet. The building has its original varying-width wood flooring under the carpet. The narrow

stairs in the corner are original and are constructed of wood planks made of chestnut. Period doors and locks still remain at the lower-level exits.

The keeping room is one of the original features of this building (c. 1795), as is the old kitchen with its seven-foot fireplace. The ironwork crane over the fireplace remains in working order. A hand-pegged wood cabinet stands next to the fireplace. Two more fireplaces, with hand-pegged mantels, grace the second-floor dining room, which was among the additions made in the early 1800s.

The courtyard is of special interest, having been paved with more than 4,000 hand-made bricks from a gristmill operating in nearby Monrovia at the time. The original grindstone from that gristmill remains a unique feature of the courtyard. The smokehouse located there also dates back to the 1795 period.

According to information in the Historic Society file, Franklin and Eleanor Rappold purchased this property in 1964. In the 1980s, the building was expanded with the addition of a living area in the back. Subsequently, it was purchased by attorney Gordon Kindness and his wife Isabella, who gave it the name "House of Kindness" and featured the sale of Scottish imports there in the 1990s. While this was considered by the town government to be "a non-conforming use" of such a property, an exception was allowed in this case.[20] A similar exception was granted in 2003, when it was sold to Sharon Press, who has opened a lamp/lighting shop there. The new shop, called "The Plug Inn," has a lighting showroom and offers lamps, crystal fixtures, home lighting, and accessories.

---

[20] Zoning restrictions in New Market are discussed in Chapter 21.

Before Mrs. Kindness left New Market, following the death of her husband, she turned over much of the historical information about the National Hotel to Sharon, who graciously provided it for inclusion here.
- JFS

Former National Pike Inn at 9-11 W. Main St. – Landmark Plaque Number 261: This is a two-story Federal-style brick building with original pine and chestnut floors, fireplaces, and door locks. It was one of the houses used as an example to add New Market to the National Register of Historic Places. The building consists of three sections built respectively in 1796, 1802, and 1804. It has stone thresholds at its front and side entrances. A carriage house and smokehouse were added in the 1830s. One of its owners, Dr. H. Hanford Hopkins, added a "widow's watch" on the roof, where he could view much of the town from above.[21]

In 1986, then owners Tom and Terry Rimel converted the home into a bed and breakfast place. Neither had done anything like running a "B&B" before. Tom was a roofer by profession, and his wife had no business experience, but she was determined to give it a try. Having raised three sons, she had come to enjoy doing the cooking and cleaning for her family and thought she could do it for their B&B guests as well. The couple already had been New Market residents when they bought this property on Main Street, which also was known as "The National Pike." (See Chapter 6, "The National Road.") So, they decided to call their B&B the "National Pike Inn."

There was much work to be done before opening the place to the public. With the help of their teen-aged sons, Tom and

---

[21] See Chaper 12 for more information about Dr. Hopkins and his remarkable family.

Terry tackled such tasks as plumbing and electrical repairs, wallpapering, painting, and general household cleaning over a period of months. They discovered that there were nine fireplaces in all, but none workable.

In preparing and furnishing their place, the Rimels received help from Edgar and Jane Rossig, who had a B&B of their own just a few doors away, and by Shirley Shaw, a local shop-owner. Mrs. Rimel chose to decorate the guest bedrooms in various styles. For example, one was of eighteenth century décor. It featured a very large, high, canopied bed. Guests there would find their own private bath just down the hall. Another large bedroom was done in the Victorian style. It had a queen-sized poster bed and an adjacent bath.

Guests in the two remaining bedrooms had to share a bathroom. There was a large (double) brass bed in the rear guest room. The other room had twin beds, thus accommodating the individual needs of guests.

Each morning at a pre-arranged time, guests would find a continental breakfast left just outside their rooms. The meal was included in the cost of the rooms, which ranged from forty-five to sixty-five dollars in 1986. If desired, Mrs. Rimel also would make dinner reservations for her guests at Mealey's Restaurant just across the road from the National Pike Inn. Guests also could choose to relax and watch television in the parlor downstairs. However, there were no TVs or telephones in the guest rooms, the theory being that B&B guests most often come to get away from their usual way of life.

The Rimels operated their B&B from 1986 until 1998, when Dr. and Mrs. Michael Morris purchased the property.

Residence at 13 W. Main St. – Landmark Plaque Number 074: This house was built in about 1800. Although it was restored in 1972, the exterior carpentry is original and is characteristic of the Federal period. It is unique in that there are seven fireplaces – three on the first floor and four on the second floor – with the original mantels. The house features a large hallway entrance and an original open stairway to the second floor. During the 1970s, Mignon M. and Edward W. Sanger owned the property. Currently, it is the site of John L. Due Antiques.

Residence at 14 W. Main St. – Landmark Plaque Number 007: The plaque next to the front door of this home points to its significance in the history of New Market. But current owners Douglas and Patricia Racine conducted their own research and even have traced their property to the first deeds recorded by Nicholas Hall on June 1, 1793. Hall sold a front lot, Lot 37, and two back lots, 104 and 105, to William Wood on that date for seven pounds. Roger Randall bought Lot 38 from Hall at the same time, for the sum of three pounds. Less than a year later, Randall sold Lot 38 to Silas Bailey for 82 pounds, a sizable profit for the time. But two years later, in November 1796, Belt Brashear paid 160 pounds for the same lot. According to a later occupant, Dr. H. Hanford Hopkins II, Dr. Brashear built this "imposing Georgian dwelling house" in about 1812. Subsequently, Brashear's son-in-law Dr. Basil Moberly used it for his office/home.

Doug Racine notes that Brashear married the granddaughter of Maryland's first governor, Thomas Johnson, and that her first cousin was married to John Quincy Adams, the sixth United States President (1825-29).

The house at 14 W. Main was built in stages on Lot 38 with what currently is the living room possibly being constructed first. The house featured large fireplaces and elaborate woodwork and furnishings that remain. For many years there were turnbuckles that were used to ring for servants. Out back were slave quarters, a smokehouse, and a bank barn, which was said to be the largest in New Market.

By 1840, Lots 38, 104, and 105 - comprising the current property at 14 W. Main - came under the same ownership. John H. M. Smith bought it in April of that year for $2,500. Land records state that the property also included: "twenty-three feet four inches of the back part of Lot 37, it being at the corner of an old shed or stable referred to in a deed given by John Burgess to John H.M. Smith in or about the year 1816 and recorded in the land records of Frederick County Court."

The property changed hands eight times during the next 100 years. Town physician Dr. H. Hanford Hopkins II and his wife, for example, rented it for a time in the early 1900s. The house was restored in 1940. Then, in October 1947, a young entrepreneur named Stoll Kemp and his wife Katherine bought the property and moved their antique shop there.[22] During their ownership of the property, Stoll regrettably removed the bell system from the house and tore down the smokehouse, slave quarters, and large barn all of which might have endured as relics of historic interest.

Kemp and his wife prospered in their business and enjoyed high standing in their community over a fifty-year period. In

[22] See "The Stoll Kemp Story" in Chapter 13.

July 1987, when he was eighty-two years of age, they sold the property to the Racines.

Doug Racine is a retired civil servant formerly with the navy. Since retiring, he says he has done many restorations, and he now has an antique store in an outbuilding at the back

The Strawberry Inn.

of his property. Among the items he has discovered in his eighteenth–century home is a long, white clay pipe that he found in the attic.

During his sixteen years in New Market, Racine has taken an active interest in town affairs and, in fact, has served four years as head of the Planning and Zoning Commission.

Strawberry Inn at 17 W. Main St. - Landmark Plaque Number 111: This house was built initially in 1837-1840, with the front portion being added in 1870. It has a Victorian parlor and working fireplace. The building also features attractive dentil molding on the exterior as well as hand-stenciled doors and stenciling on either side of the staircase to the second floor. Former Mayor Franklin Smith, who was born and raised in New Market, made this his home for thirty-six years before selling it in 1973 to Edgar William Rossig, Jr., and his wife Jane. Edgar retired at that time from Westinghouse, where he had designed televisions. He was

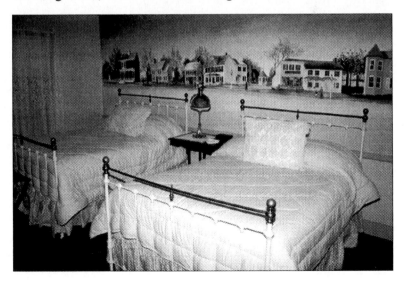

only fifty-five then. He and Jane were determined to start a new and exciting chapter in their lives.

The Rossigs previously lived in Pennsylvania, New Jersey, Massachusetts, and Indiana, but they learned about New Market and its antiques while they were in New Jersey. They liked "the uniqueness of the houses, the town itself, the preservation, and the history," Jane recalls. This would be where they would begin a new career.

Edgar and Jane started by completely restoring their new home, and they added a bathroom off of each bedroom. Later in 1973, with the restoration work completed, they established it as a bed and breakfast inn. Jane notes that they did not need to put up a sign at first: "People just came and knocked on our front door." The inn has four guest rooms, each of which is furnished with attractive antiques. Guests seem to appreciate the fact that each bedroom has its own private bath. Also, they have the choice of two rooms with queen-sized beds, one with two double beds, or another room with one full-sized bed. Breakfast, normally served in the first-floor dining room, also can be enjoyed café-style on the back porch when the weather is inviting. In addition, guests may enjoy the convenience of evening dining right across the street at Mealey's Restaurant.

Jane recalls that a descendant of the Plummer Family, so important in the founding of New Market, once stayed at her B&B while going to a jousting tournament in Walkersville, Maryland. At the time, he was living on the state's eastern shore. The Rossigs both took an avid interest in the town's history. Edgar served as the first president of the New Market Historical Society, a position subsequently taken over by their son, Edgar "Bud" Rossig III.

In 1992, Edgar Rossig, Jr., put his considerable talents as a carpenter to work and built a very attractive gazebo behind the Strawberry Inn. It became, and still remains, a wonderful place for family, friends, and B&B guests to relax and enjoy the quiet beauty of the inn's back yard.

Edgar passed away in 1997, but Jane continues to operate Strawberry Inn as a B&B with the help of her fellow innkeepers, their son Bud and his wife Sonja. They take considerable pride in its being the oldest B&B in Frederick County.

William Wood Home at 20 W. Main St. – (No Landmark Plaque): Wood built this home on some of the property he purchased in 1793 from Nicholas Hall. The first section of the house sits on the left, and there also was a smokehouse as well as a summer kitchen in back. Over the years there have been additions, and the building has been used as a private home, including the home of a doctor, as a post office for the town, and as a private school. For a time, it also had the questionable reputation as an inn for the "entertainment of gentlemen."

Like 14 W. Main, the home became one of the first antique shops in New Market. In the fall of 2002, Robert Esterly bought the place. He has been in the antique business elsewhere since 1974 and calls his shop "Robert Esterly Antiques."

Residence/Shop at 25-27 W. Main St., Formerly "Mymanor" – Landmark Plaque Number 029: This property is unique in many respects. To begin with, it is the only stone house in town. Richard Roberts, a Quaker, built the house. He bought the land from one of New Market's founders, Nicholas Hall, on 9 September 1794 for seven pounds ten shillings. Roberts erected the two-story structure of fieldstone. It is a country house of the Federal Period. Over the years, subsequent owners erected additional wings and made other changes. The property, in fact, has had an interesting history with respect to its structural changes, its ownership, and its uses over the past two centuries.

The original stone house featured a single room on the first floor with a fireplace at each end and a staircase winding upward to the second floor, where there was a room and a half, and to the attic above. Near the back door was a stone well that had been dug by hand.

The first addition, a kitchen, was to the rear of the house in

1798. This wing, constructed of brick, has two bays and may have had a two-story porch at one time, but the lower porch long-since has been enclosed as living space. The country kitchen has a very large brick fireplace, a beamed ceiling, brick walls, and random-width plank flooring. The large dining and living rooms have the same types of flooring and beamed ceilings. Altogether, the house has three working fireplaces plus a Franklin fireplace in the study.

Subsequent additions in 1817 to the east of the original stone house included a two-story frame structure (with three bays on each level) and an adjacent one-story single-bay wing which has been used at times as a shop. There also were various outbuildings, several of which have been preserved over the years. They include an old cabin, more recently used as a pool house; an original smokehouse and original outhouse; and a five-bay carriage house in the rear of the lot.

This property belonged to Richard Roberts and then to his heirs until 1817 when it was sold to Henry Maynard for $2,500. He is said to have turned the house into a place for selling groceries and dry goods. Maynard sold it to Jesse Wright, Jr., two years later for the same amount. Wright built a tannery shop behind the house. Rachel Smith took over the property in 1837. She is believed to have had a considerable amount of property in New Market and was known also for possessing a large number of slaves. In fact, she converted the tannery to slave quarters. When Rachel died in 1842, the property passed to her grandson, Philemon Smith Anderson and, later, to his heirs.[23]

This same property was deeded to Martha F. Hammond in 1863, to Lloyd C. Belt in 1865, to Dr. Isaac N. Wood and Lydia Wood in 1867, and then to George and Sarah Sponseller in 1868. It remained in the Sponseller Family until 1961, when it was deeded to John M. Prosser and Ina E. Prosser for $30,000. For many years thereafter, it was known in town as "The Prosser House." Subsequently, the Ellison Family owned it.

---

[23] See Chapter 8, "Slavery in New Market."

Richard and Susan Buckel bought the property from the Ellisons in 1984. The Buckels operated an antique shop there and called it "Mymanor." Following the loss of her husband, Susan Buckel decided to close the shop, put the property up for sale, and leave New Market. The current owners, Glenn and Katherine Berkhousen, bought it from her in December 2002.

The following unsigned notes describing the home were found by the Berkhousens. It is possible that a former owner wrote these notes in anticipation of selling the property:

> *...Inside one finds a center hall flanked by rooms with low, beamed ceilings, wide planked floors, and wonderful bay windows. A small quaint country brick kitchen complete with a fireplace opens on an eighteenth-century dining room with original hand-blown glass windows. A second door opens upon a spacious family room, originally a porch, now a charming beamed room steeped in character looking out upon a fenced brick patio, boxwood garden, and a 150-year-old cabin in original condition.*
>
> *A front parlor features a typical Federal period fireplace and a four-walled mural depicting the original town of New Market done by Virginia Jacobs McLaughlin. Across the hall is the antique shop devoted to English and American sporting art from the 19th and 20th centuries of extraordinary quality. The entire home is furnished in period pieces along with horse and dog painting and art objects.*

The Berkhousens are very interested in the historic preservation of the home and currently are busy refurbishing it. They plan to reopen the adjacent shop and will feature a collection of antiques from Germany.

Victorian Manor at 33 W. Main St. – Landmark Plaque Number 194: Nicholas Hall sold this land (which includes Lot 32–99B plus thirteen feet of Lot 31-98) to Caleb Pancoast for 120 pounds on January 18, 1804, after which it changed hands several times and saw use as a blacksmith shop. According to the current owner, Gene Rooney, this two-story, nine-room Victorian-style home was built sometime between 1880 and 1883 on the foundation of the earlier blacksmith shop. A horse shed and tack room were located on the back of the property. The Victorian Manor has a slate roof, brick gables, shutters, stone window-caps and sills, and an inviting front porch with Victorian ornamentation.

Rooney came to New Market from Arlington, Virginia, in 1976. He had worked in the jewelry business in Washington, D.C., and decided to start his own shop in New Market selling antique jewelry. His wife Carol Ann Rooney was his partner in business until she passed away. Gene recently decided to give up the business after twenty-eight years, finding it too difficult to carry on without his partner-wife. He says that he currently is disposing of his inventory.

Main Street Antiques at 45-47 W. Main St. – Landmark Plaque Number 160: This structure evolved over the years, with the easternmost section being the oldest. It was built in about 1810. Soon thereafter came the log structure in the middle. The smaller section on the west side was not added until 1960. Monroe Free and his wife, Hilda Brashear Free, who was named Acting Postmaster of New Market in 1961, lived in the center portion of the home and the new section next to the alley became the town's post office until Mrs. Free retired as Postmaster in 1978.

James and Violet Moore, the proprietors of Main Street Antiques, bought the property in 1995. Their shop specializes in old country store items, vintage clothing, veterinary items, and other antique articles. After closing its doors in 2003 during needed renovations, the antique shop reopened for business in September 2004.

The 1812 House, at 48 W. Main St. – Landmark Plaque Number 146: William and Colleen Shook purchased this house in 1982 from Nina Lee, the widow of E. Brooke Lee, who had been a highly successful and well-known land developer in Montgomery County as well as Frederick County, Maryland. Mrs. Lee had owned the property only since 1975 before selling it to the Shooks, who then established their own shop, specializing in fine porcelain, furniture, and many unique decorating items.

Built about 1812, or possibly as early as 1795, by New Market founder William Plummer, this house has had a succession of many owners. The exterior is gray stucco over brick, with attractive dentils. Known previously as "The Old Silver Shop," it also served earlier as a shoe factory, wrought iron nail shop, button factory, and tannery. There were additions to the home in 1864 and 1869, according to the 1975 application for landmark status. The house sits on a large lot, and there is a very old brick smokehouse just to the rear.

Upon entering the 1812 House, customers may take note of some unusual items in a small showroom to the left, but the large front room may steal their immediate attention. It features two impressive brick fireplaces on one wall, on either side of a large, oval mirror. Tall glass showcases line two of the remaining walls. They are filled with an assortment of blue and white porcelain pieces dating from 1830 to 1845. Just three steps down, in the middle of the shop, there is an additional showroom containing a few furniture items and other antiques.

Hearth and Eagle Farmhouse at 5921 Boyers Mill Rd. – Landmark Plaque Number 046: This house was built in the 1790s on a farm just west of where the Town of New Market was being established. To get there, one takes a right turn off of Boyers Mill Road, proceeding through the woods along a country lane. The brick, Federal-style house soon comes into view, in the open but marked by a beautiful tree in front, as well as a gracious driveway and lovely lawn. The Hearth and Eagle Farmhouse is noted for its fine woodwork and paneling, two chimneys, and five fireplaces - including a corner fireplace and also a very large walk-in-type kitchen fireplace. The latter has a huge mantle cut from a log that is

twelve to fifteen inches thick. Restorations took place in the 1960s and 1970s. Beautiful paneling above the mantel was crafted from old shutters. According to the present owners, the fireplaces originally had elaborate iron fire-backs, forged in the 1700s, but they are no longer there.

Perhaps the most unusual features of the house are its two front entrances. They are side by side, and each has its own steps and black front door, but at different levels. The right door is higher than the left. The reason is that the house was built in two stages. Sources stating that this house may have been built in 1791 evidently must be referring to the first part of the house. Abner Miller is believed to have constructed the second section of the house in 1796. His initials and that date are inscribed at the top of the chimney on the left portion of the house.

Members of the Clay Family resided here during the nineteenth century. Thomas A. and Julie L. Vogl are the current owners, having purchased the property in 1998 from interior designer Edith Elliott. The Vogls live on twelve acres of the original farm and lease an additional four acres where they keep their horses. Elliott bought the property in 1965 and did much to maintain the historic authenticity of the home. It was she who came up with the name "Hearth and Eagle," after finding an iron plaque of an eagle on a chimney there.

CHAPTER 4

The Utz Mercantile - Now the New Market General Store

Background

The building at 26 West Main has its own history. To begin with, it is really five buildings in one. The first was a one-room log cabin in the 1790s. The two rooms now in front were added in about 1830, and a second-story log structure was built in about 1850. The original one-story portion was torn down in 1881 and replaced with the two stories that now

exist on the same stone foundation, which was said to be solid and "dry as a bone."

Town zoning that went into effect in 1979 allowed for one additional building on the property, and some further enlargement of the structure was permitted in the 1990s. The property has been used as a trading post, a butcher shop, post office, barbershop, millinery, candy store, Greyhound bus stop, and antique shop. It also was rented and used as a grocery.

The Utz's

The first prominent storeowner at 26 West Main was a remarkable entrepreneur, Silas Kelly Utz, who established a general store there known as "Utz Mercantile." Silas Utz and his brother Samuel Utz, who started a hotel in New Market, were descendants of Daniel Utz, who fled Germany in 1752 because of religious persecution and came to Pennsylvania. Some of Daniel's descendants, including Silas and Samuel, later settled in New Market, Maryland.

Silas K. Utz, Dr.
Dealer in
Dry Goods, Notions, Groceries, Boots, and

Shoes, Oils, Paints, and General
Merchandise

C. & P. Phone 2-F

Photo From Cynthia
Utz Harding of
Pasadena, California,
Courtesy of
Bud Rossig

This is a copy of an historic sign for Utz Mercantile business in the New Market General Store. Note that the store had one of the first telephones of the era from the Chesapeake & Potomac Telephone Company.

Married and the father of eleven children, Samuel Utz also was a minister at the Bush Creek Church of the Brethren, in nearby Monrovia, where he is buried.

Utz Family Reunion

Some 225 descendants of Daniel Utz came to Monrovia, Maryland in 2003 for their fiftieth family reunion. The event was held at the Bush Creek Church of the Brethren, where Samuel Utz once preached. Various generations traveled from far and near to meet one another, to share their memorabilia, pictures, and recollections, and also to enjoy traditional German food and music.

A Succession of Owners

Subsequent owners of the general store included Lorenzo Grimes, Andrew J. Zimmerman, Robert and Bonnie Harrington, Harrison and Ruth Metz, Bill Armstrong, and John and Karen Carrier. Zimmerman bought the store in 1918 and operated it for twenty-five years. He installed the first gasoline pumps in town. An old photograph shows him standing with his dog between the two pumps in front of the store. (See Chapter 11.) His family took over the property in 1943 until selling it to the Metzes. They moved to New Market in 1942 and operated it for almost forty years (1949-1988) as "Metz's Country Store." During this period it comprised a complete grocery store, and it was open seven days a week, except for Christmas Day. Ruth Metz well recalls those years and notes that she and her husband introduced antiques to the variety of goods sold there, as is still the practice currently.

Sophie Myers remembers living in the building with her husband Nelson Myers, Jr., while the Zimmermans owned it.

"Our oldest boy was born there in 1946," she recalls. Speaking about the Town of New Market, Sophie observes, "It was a nice place to live; I'll tell you that." When the building was sold, the Myers Family moved to Ijamsville, where Nelson served as its last postmaster until the post office there closed in 1982.

For Karen Carrier, a more recent proprietor of the store, it was more than just a business opportunity that brought her to New Market. When she was growing up in Jerseyville, Illinois, Karen's father had owned two general stores. Both were named after her: "Kay's Variety." Each time, their house was collocated with the  store. Karen recalls that she always wanted to live next to a soda fountain, and she always wanted to have her own general store. When the New Market store became available in 1997, Karen and her husband John Carrier found the opportunity irresistible.

The general store had been empty for almost three years, and it even was condemned at one point. The Carriers made extensive renovations in 1997 but were careful to maintain such features as the wooden beams, original floors and ceilings, and much of the shelving from years ago. It has been Karen's goal to make the place as authentic as possible. Modern-day restrictions sometimes interfere however. For example, the Health Department will not allow a pickle barrel or wood stove in the store. Likewise, the town zoning authorities have greatly restricted dining facilities/service there. Nevertheless, Karen maintained a little kitchen in the back of the store with five small tables where townspeople and visitors alike could rest and enjoy some homemade soups, chili, special sandwiches prepared to order, fresh coffees, or soft drinks from the fountain. The store was open every day except Wednesdays during this period.

Customers

For many years, New Market mayors, council members, and other town residents have frequented the general store, especially on weekdays. Sales and delivery people likewise find it a convenient place to stop for lunch or to meet a client. On weekends, the place often is packed with visitors enjoying a day's outing in New Market. Frequently, they bring their children along. Usually less interested in antiques than their parents, the youngsters find the General Store to be a bit of a haven, where they can savor an ice cream cone, fudge, licorice, or gumballs and maybe find an unusual toy.

Visitors to the New Market General Store come from near and far, it seems. "Maggie" stopped by one Tuesday in the summer of 2003 with her sixteen-year-old sister and her mother, who is a teacher at Deer Crossing Elementary School just west of New Market. Almost three months old, Maggie seemed to enjoy the outing.

Meanwhile, at another table, Kirsten and Chris Shilakes were having a great time with their daughters Jocelyn (3 ½) and Isabelle (2). They had journeyed to New Market from their home in Mill Valley, California, near San Francisco. It was just one stop they were making on a National Geographic tour of scenic small towns throughout the United States. Chris explained that they already had covered 6,000 miles on their five-month tour of thirty-one states. While in New Market, the Shilakes Family stayed at the Strawberry Inn Bed and Breakfast. Mrs. Shilakes mentioned walking down Gallery Lane from there with her two little girls and boasted of her purchase of two lovely glass decanters at a local shop.

On the wall behind the cash register, near the front door, glass jars full of various hard candies line five very long shelves. Children love to pick out their favorite flavors and colors, just as they did in such general stores a century ago.

As was the case with general stores of yesteryear, customers find much more here than food. The colorful Old World Christmas Ornaments are a special feature, along with hand-made quilts, and several adjacent rooms full of antique items, special books, and collectibles. Customers seem to enjoy going down the steps (to the right after entering the store) to discover one little room after the next.

One of the local antique dealers has described the General Store as the "Jewel of New Market." Certainly, it is a unique attraction and a rallying place for visitors.

Mealey's Restaurant in 2004 Photo (With "Hunting Doll" Shop to the Left.

CHAPTER 5

The Utz Hotel,
Now Mealey's Restaurant

The building at 8 W. Main Street has seen many forms, and numerous owners, over its colorful history of more than 200 years. John Roberts purchased the land in 1793, and a small stone structure was erected there prior to 1800. (A portion of the original stone wall is still visible inside.) Roberts made a small store and tavern out of it, and it subsequently became an inn within an L-shaped, two-story building. A third-story was added in the mid-1800s, whereupon the structure assumed its current appearance in the late Federal style of architecture, with bedrooms on the upper floors at that time.

One of the most interesting features of the old hotel was its open courtyard with the outdoor pump where fresh water could be drawn for guests and their horses. In those days, there was no more important commodity for weathered travelers and their animals coming off a long day's trek of seven or eight miles. There were "drovers" driving their sheep or cattle to market, "draymen" with their heavily loaded carts, and travelers aiming to explore the new frontier.

Prior to the Civil War, the building was sold to E.T. Hilton and J. T. Lowe. Although it was called "The Hilton Hotel," it was not connected in any way with the well-known national chain of Hilton Hotels.

New Market Hotel Courtyard. Dr. H.H. Hopkins II 1885 Photo, Courtesy of Bud Rossig.

Samuel Utz bought the building on 1 January 1899 and renamed it the Utz Hotel. He turned over its operation to his son Charles, who made a successful business of it by catering to traveling salesmen (called "drummers" in those days) who, by then, were traveling by rail instead of by horseback or stagecoach. He provided passenger pick-up service to the railroad station in nearby Monrovia in a manner similar to our modern-day airport courtesy vans from major hotels and motels. Monrovia had the railroad station, but New Market - only a mile away - had the food and lodging these drummers required.

Meanwhile, with technology advancing, further changes took place in this historic structure. It was in 1883 that the first local offices of the regional Chesapeake and Potomac (C. & P.) Telephone Company set up operations in Frederick County, and the number of local subscribers, including some in New Market, quickly reached 200. Modern

The Historic Utz Hotel, Family Photo From Cynthia Utz Harding, Courtesy of Bud Rossig.

communications had arrived. The telephone lines had reached New Market, and a temporary location was needed to accommodate the exchange there. A small structure adjacent to the Utz Hotel was selected to house the telephone exchange. The characteristic Bell Telephone symbol can be seen on photographs of the Utz Hotel in the 1880s, hanging on that structure just to the left of the hotel. For modern-day telephone subscribers, it might be interesting to note that the annual cost of phone service in 1883 was thirty-six dollars for residences and fifty dollars for businesses.

During the following century, this historic building continued to be adaptable to the changing needs of this small town. Carl Mealey and his wife Nettie bought it in 1918 and ran it as a hotel for twenty-two years. As the story goes, Mr. Mealey frequently would meet traveling salesmen arriving on local trains, act as their chauffeur on business calls, and then drive them to his hotel for a night's lodging. Then, in 1940, the Mealeys' son Dick and his wife Frances took over, stopped renting rooms, and established a family restaurant there. They were the good people that gave the place the name it still has and its reputation for fine dining. Mealeys went from being a hotel or inn to a restaurant of some note and great popularity.

The main dining room was built in the 1960s. The area previously served as a courtyard with balconies. This dining area has come to be known as "The Pump Room" because of its historic feature, the original wood pump. No longer operative, the pump is still in the same position as it was years ago, as seen in an 1885 photograph.

In the 1960s, my family and I were on an outing from our home in Rockville, and we came to New Market. We had the pleasure of dining at Mealey's and enjoying a wonderful, family-style dinner. I remember talking with Mrs. Mealey. She was very gracious, and I also remember that each table had a decanter of homemade dandelion wine on it, now a thing of the past, of course.   - JFS

After Dick Mealey passed away, Frances Mealey continued to manage the restaurant until 1981, when James Jeffries and his wife Fran bought it. They owned it only until 1988, when Pat and Jose Salaverri purchased it. Like many others, this couple had discovered New Market's charm during a country excursion. Both had been involved in food service while in Annapolis, Maryland, and were anxious to operate a restaurant of their own. After a few years, they saw the need to carry out major renovations to bring the place up to code, improve air conditioning, and achieve a more convenient layout of rooms. Offices, for example, were moved to the third floor. Throughout this effort, however, the Salaverris took great pains to preserve the historic nature and character of the building.

In addition to the Pump Room for main dining, Mealeys now has a small dining room, called "The Utz Room," for private parties, additional dining areas on the first floor, as well as the second-floor "John Roberts Room," named for the pioneer who first bought the property site. The latter is a large, very attractive dining room. "Man, what a view!" Jose exclaims, expressing his satisfaction with its five front windows overlooking Main Street. Gazing out these windows, diners can imagine what the same view might have been like some 200 years ago, with horses, wagons, and livestock passing by.

Under the direction of the Salaverris, Mealey's Restaurant has achieved great popularity and considerable recognition for its fine cuisine, refined atmosphere, and excellent service. For many years now, it has ranked among the top five restaurants in Frederick County as judged by **Frederick Magazine**. The owners, however, measure their restaurant's quality by the satisfaction of its customers. Jose puts it this way: "We are as good as the last meal we served to you."

Dinner is served in this historic establishment on Tuesdays through Saturdays from 3 p.m. to 9 p.m. and on Sundays from noon to 8 p.m. Lunch is available on Fridays and Saturdays only from 11:30 a.m. to 2 p.m. The Sunday brunch, from 10 a.m. to 2 p.m., is especially popular with New Market visitors and residents alike.

Reflecting on his years in New Market, along with his wife Pat, Jose points out that it is easier to get to know people in a small community such as this, adding: "Our seventeen years in this town have been incredibly enjoyable."

Nineteenth Century Bicycle at New Market Hotel. Hopkins Photo, 1885, Courtesy of Bud Rossig.

CHAPTER 6

The National Road

In the earliest years of our nation, road construction was not funded through taxation. Public lotteries often were held to raise monies for this purpose, as was the case with the building of north-south Route 75 just to the east of New Market. In other cases, a privately funded "turnpike" was constructed, and tolls were demanded of travelers using them. Those using these special roads periodically had to stop at gates made of logs or wood spears, called "pikes," to pay the designated toll. The gates were turned open once the toll was paid. Thus the term "turnpike."[24]

This was not a new idea. For example, companies in England had built turnpikes there and collected tolls for profit. Similarly, tolls were collected on a Persian military road between Syria and Babylon as long ago as 2000 BC.[25]

The first American turnpike was constructed in 1785 in Virginia. Maryland responded in 1792 with a turnpike of its own between Frederick and Cumberland. Later, the "Baltimore Pike," financed by Maryland state banks, linked Baltimore with Frederick and Cumberland. Segments of it were known variously as the "Bank Road," "Baltimore Pike," or "National Pike."

During his presidency (1801-1809), Thomas Jefferson and his Treasury Secretary Albert Gallatin saw the need for a

---

[24] *Worldbook 2001, Vol. 19, 518-519.*
[25] *Worldbook 2001, Vol. 4, 519.*

national road that would extend from Cumberland all the way to St. Louis, Missouri. Such a road would promote westward settlement from the eastern seaboard to the banks of the Mississippi River. The U.S. Congress approved the undertaking in 1806, the banks financed it, and the work commenced in 1811.[26] The road would be hard-surfaced, thirty feet in width with a good stone surface and a cleared right-of-way on each side.[27, 28]

Stone bridges likewise had to be built, and they had to be strong enough for the heavily loaded Conestoga wagons of the time. The Jug Bridge erected over the Monocacy River near Frederick is typical of the stone bridges built during this period. It was completed in 1809. After 133 years, this stone bridge with its four arches had to be replaced. But the large, ten-foot-high, ten-ton demijohn (jug) that adorned it has been preserved as a monument along Route 144 east of the city.

The road project progressed as far as Vandalia, Illinois, in 1839, covering 700 miles. As a result, Baltimore, Frederick, and even the new little town of New Market were linked with the nation's Midwest for purposes of trade, travel, exploration, and emigration. The road was named "The Great National Pike" in the beginning but later became known as the National Road. For a long period, it was the primary road leading west. Accordingly, it was described at times as "the road that built the nation," and it became the first federally funded highway. Its importance continued throughout the 1800s in spite of increasing competition from railroads starting to be constructed in the 1830s. On the other hand, the development of the automobile, and especially Henry Ford's first Model T in 1908, boosted the importance and popularity of the National Road.

---

[26] *Worldbook 2001,* Vol. 14, 60.

[27] Karl Raitz (editor), *The National Road,* Johns Hopkins University Press, Baltimore and London, 1996, 171-176, 283.

[28] Vera F. Rollo, *Your Maryland,* Maryland Historical Press, Lanham, Md., 3rd ed revised 1976, 196-203.

Travel was slow along this route in its earliest years. But, as travel increased, so did the need for stopover places, with taverns and inns, animal pens, wagon facilities, and repair services. New Market was just that sort of place. The town prospered from its strategic location along this route. Also, residents, no doubt, were fascinated by the daily procession of small wagons, coaches, teams of four to six horses pulling Conestoga wagons, or by drovers herding pigs, sheep, cows, and other animals down Main Street. Children sat on logs or doorsteps to watch the daily parade. Innkeepers and guests swapped stories, and travelers brought news obtained during their journeys. On the other hand, strains from travel or over-imbibing sometimes resulted in street brawls.

> In Frederick County, the National Road traces Maryland Route 144, US 40, and US 40A. As it meanders through the Appalachian Mountains and Ohio Valley, it follows Interstate 70 and US 40.

All-American Status

On 13 June 2002, the U.S. Department of Transportation recognized the importance of the National Road by awarding it special status as an "All-American Road." This award, acknowledging its significance as the first major east-west road in the U.S., is intended to foster tourism and preservation of facilities constructed in the 1800s, including tollhouses, gates, and associated structures that have survived. This new designation also should facilitate the awarding of grants for museums, signs, and the acquisition of properties along the road for preservation purposes.[29]

An effort recently was mounted to request that the U.S. Postal Service issue a commemorative stamp in 2006 to celebrate the 200th anniversary of the authorization of the National Road.

[29] *Frederick News-Post,* Frederick, Md., June 21, 2002, A-4.

Town officials made the most of New Market's key location along the National Road by holding a special ribbon-cutting ceremony there on 8 May 2003.[30] Federal, state, and local representatives attended, as did many of the townspeople. Maryland's Lt. Governor Michael Steele highlighted the occasion by driving a horse-drawn wagon down Main Street. The event commemorated the town's colorful past and its historic service to travelers along this "All-American Road."

The portion of the Old National Road that runs through New Market (i.e., Main Street) also was designated as a "linear park." As such, it became part of the Federal Park extending through a number of states all the way to Indiana.

[30] *Frederick News-Post,* Frederick, Md., May 9, 2003, A-1.

CHAPTER 7

The Coming of the Railroad

The Railroad Never Came to New Market - The Folks in New Market Had to Come to the Railroad!

The Baltimore and Ohio Railroad was the first railroad in the United States. It was chartered in 1827 just two years after a man by the name of John Stevens put together and demonstrated the first U.S. steam locomotive.[31] Steam was used to power railroad locomotives until about 1900, when some electric engines were introduced, with diesel-electric locomotives replacing most steam locomotives by the mid-1900s. In the early 1800s, however, teams of horses pulled the railroad's first cars.

Construction of the Baltimore and Ohio (B&O) Railroad began on 4 July 1828 and extended from Baltimore to Frederick, Maryland, during the very early 1830s.[32] The rail line passed just south of New Market through the nearby village of Monrovia. A small railroad station thus was established in Monrovia, not in New Market. It must have made sense at the time, probably because of the plentiful supply of water from Bush Creek. Local area maps illustrate how closely the rail line follows alongside Bush Creek. In 1840, a watering station for the steam locomotives was built in Monrovia. The railroad station in Monrovia also provided

---

[31] *Brittanica Micropaedia Ready Reference,* Vol. 9, 15th ed., 2002, Chicago, 903.
[32] T.J.C. Williams and Folger McKinsey, *History of Frederick County,* Regional Publications Co., Baltimore, 1967 Reprint of 1910 ed, Vol. I., 152-153, 229-233.

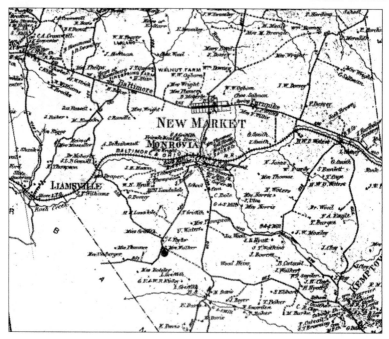

New Market Area Map From 1873 Titus Atlas.

much-needed rail service to the mills and other nearby enterprises.

From Baltimore, construction of the railroad bed proceeded westward through Ellicott City and on to Mt. Airy, only seven miles east of New Market, but the hills in and around Mt. Airy, and especially Parr's Ridge, presented special problems. It became necessary to develop a series of four inclined planes so that trains could ascend and descend the ridge gradually. The planes were not nearly as steep as the contours of the hills being traversed. Planes 1 and 2 ascended the ridge from the east to the Ridgeville crest. Planes 3 and 4 descended from the ridge toward the west.

Initially, trains were pulled over Parr's Ridge by teams of draft horses hitched to the rail cars by steel cables.[33, 34] Eventually, engine power replaced horsepower. Later, work was completed on excavation of a tunnel, allowing trains to bypass the ridge as they do today.

An old railroad building still stands along Rt. 144 just west of its intersection with Woodville Road. Until recent years, it bore a sign marking the location of "Plane No. 4." Currently, a modified version of the sign can be seen hanging across the road at Dorsey's garage.

The work force for this great project consisted mostly of newly arrived immigrants to the U.S., mainly of Irish descent, along with local laborers and some slaves. The work was hard, and the relationships between these workers and the contractors who hired them were sometimes turbulent. There were uprisings, such as a work rebellion in June/July 1831 over non-payment of salaries at a site near what is now Sykesville, Maryland, about 17 miles east of New Market.[35]

The New Market area itself was the scene of a more violent eruption on 14-15 August 1831. Local residents were able to quell this flare-up, between black laborers/slaves and Irish workers, only after one person died and many were injured seriously.[36] The work of these B&O "trackmen" nevertheless proceeded despite such interruptions. They extended the railroad bed westward and laid the track.

Rail construction followed Bush Creek from Mt. Airy, through Monrovia, and all the way to where Bush Creek empties into the Monocacy River at the Frederick Junction, which is near the Monocacy National Battlefield. From

---

[33] Ibid
[34] *World Book,* 2002 ED, Chicago, Vol. 16, 114-117.
[35] Matthew E. Mason, *Labor History,* New York: Aug. 1998. Vol. 39, Iss. 3; pg. 253, 37 pgs
[36] Ibid

there, the B&O Railroad continues southwest through Buckeystown and all the way to Point of Rocks before heading northwest along the C&O Canal to Brunswick, Maryland, and Harper's Ferry, West Virginia.

Traveling west from Monrovia, the next rail stop was the small village of Ijamsville, named after its founder and first postmaster, Plummer Ijams, Jr. On 13 March 1832, all the villagers turned out to welcome the first train to stop at the Monrovia Station. The train consisted of four cars traveling on rails with one horse pulling each rail car. Fresh horses were made available at specified points along the route.

Residents from Monrovia and nearby New Market no doubt had a similar celebration during this period, as did the City of Frederick (then known as Fredericktown). They were delighted with this major new development in transportation and the services it would bring. Travelers could move more quickly to distant places. Farmers could deliver their products to distant markets more expeditiously. Furthermore, local residents could experience improvements in the quality of life. For example, residents in Frederick or New Market could enjoy fresh oysters shipped in the morning from Baltimore that same evening.

The railroad station in Monrovia was a key facility for local farmers shipping livestock and grain to market. The facility also served an adjacent cannery. But passengers from New Market had to be shuttled to the station. Salesmen staying in New Market hotels, for example, often would be picked up and returned to the station by coach. It was not unlike the hotel/motel shuttle bus service provided today at major airports except that horses pulled the coaches back then.

Baltimore-Frederick Rail Service Inaugurated

On a Thursday morning, 1 December 1831, a train of four railroad cars left Pratt Street in Baltimore at about 7:15 and made its way to a depot in Frederick.[37] A single horse pulled each of the cars, and the lead car, one of the best available, was named "The Frederick." Passengers included the Governor of Maryland, Mayor of Baltimore, and a Supreme Court judge, as well as railroad company officials. Following a celebration and dinner in Frederick, they made the return trip for a total of 120 miles in one day – a striking accomplishment for the time. Even more remarkable was the announcement that regular service from Frederick to Baltimore would commence only two days later. The schedule called for trains to leave Frederick at 9:30 a.m. daily. This service began that Saturday, 3 December 1831.

The railroad continued to be vital to the development of this region throughout the nineteenth century and, of course, provided vital services during the Civil War. Its importance continued through most of the twentieth century, especially before the development of the interstate highway system. New Market resident Kenneth Valentino relates his own observations concerning the latter part of the 1900s:

> *The railroad was a large part of the County infrastructure up into the 1980s. The section of the CSX tracks past Mt. Airy and New Market is part of the old main line that was double track from Point of Rocks to Baltimore until Hurricane Agnes, in the early seventies, wiped out much of the line in various spots. Even when we moved here in 1979, bridges were still out and roads closed because of that hurricane, and some were not replaced until the early 1980s.*

People in the New Market area, as elsewhere in the United States and especially in rural communities, enjoyed watching

[37] T.J.C. Williams and Folger McKinsey, *History of Frederick County,* Regional Publications Co., Baltimore, 1967 Reprint of 1910 ed., Vol. I., 229-233.

the trains passing by with their seemingly endless chain of cars. Many were passenger trains in years past, but freight trains abounded in more recent times. This trend was due largely to the development of the interstate highway system and to the increased popularity of air travel.

Betty (Davis) Jeffers recalls growing up not far from the railroad station in Monrovia. She says, "We had to watch our clotheslines, with all that black smoke coming from passing trains." Betty recalls going to the train station with her father to pick up baby chicks that they would raise so that they would be able to have some chicken broilers to eat during the days of wartime rationing. She also remembers hobos hopping off freight trains and coming to her house to beg for food.

Railroad buffs sometimes reflect on the bygone days. Ken Valentino, for example, recently recounted some of his memories:

> *One thing I always enjoyed were the trains on East Street in Frederick. Trains ran up and down East Street almost every day. The local ran past Frederick Brickworks, to the Farmers Co-Op, and so forth over on and just past East Patrick Street. The train went past Tauraso's Restaurant through the end of East Street. (East Street ended at East Patrick Street then.) The train went back out of town over Route 26, then through Woodsboro and on to Union Bridge, or down along the route of the new MARC Line over to Point of Rocks.*

> *The railroad and farming were huge parts of Frederick County at one time. Brunswick was a huge*

yard, when I was younger, with repair shops and a roundhouse, a large classification yard, and an AMTRAK stop. Point of Rocks was an important stop along the Main Lines from D.C. and Baltimore, where they converged. It was an AMTRAK stop until a decade or so ago.

Trains that bypassed New Market in favor of nearby Monrovia and Ijamsville in the 1830s have long since bypassed those stops as well. The significance of the railroad to the general area over the past 170 years in terms of the many jobs and services provided was profound.

Railroad Overpass in Nearby Monrovia Just South of New Market (2002 photo).

This closeup of the 1873 Titus Map shows how the north-south road from New Market to Monrovia (i.e., Green Valley Road) goes under the B&O Railroad overpass shown in the above photo.

CHAPTER 8

Slavery in New Market

One must understand that Maryland was a border state on the issue of slavery. There were those who strongly opposed the holding of slaves, and there were slaveholders - many owning 100-200 slaves - committed to the "protection of their property." In Williams' *History of Frederick County*,[38] the author sums up the situation as follows:

> *The nullification of the fugitive slave laws by Northern States and the attitude of the Northern people made Slavery precarious in the border-states and especially in Maryland, which bordered on Pennsylvania where the anti-slavery feeling was most pronounced.*

Williams also cites specific examples of slave sales in Frederick County:

> *...Now and then in the files of Frederick papers, auction sales of slaves are noticed. In March 1855 a woman 26 years old was sold for $1,010, and her 7-year-old child for $338. The condition of this sale was that neither the mother nor child should be carried out of the State. That condition was made in many of the sales. On Nov. 3, 1858 the sale of Ex-Governor Frank Thomas' slaves took place at auction at the jail. The prices paid were considered very large. One*

[38] T.J.C. Williams and Folger McKinsey, *History of Frederick County,* Regional Publications Co., Baltimore, 1967 Reprint of 1910 ed, Vol. I., 221.

girl of eighteen years sold for $1,455.   The whole lot brought $13,257...

Prior to the U.S. Civil War, or "war of emancipation," New Market did count a significant number of African-American slaves, as well as former slaves who had been freed. They were a critical part of the local work force and contributed greatly to the success and prosperity of their masters and the local community. Students of today read about the dark days of this country's past when slavery was allowed. Approximately 150 years later, it may be difficult for some to realize how human beings could be treated as just property. The situation is characterized to a degree by what one of the founders of New Market, Nicholas Hall, wrote in his last will and testament of 9 May 1820.[39] Here are just a few excerpts:

> *...I give my Negro boy Ben to my grandson Nicholas Hall Stickley to serve until December 1st 1835 and then to be free and discharged from slavery.*

> *...I give my Negro boy William to my grandson Nicholas Hall to serve until the 1st day of December 1840 and then to be free and discharged from slavery.*

> *...I give to my granddaughter Elizabeth Iams Hall my Negro girl Charity to serve until December1st 1838 and then to be free and discharged from slavery, and the issue of this said Charity born during this time of servitude to be free at the following ages: males at thirty-one and females at twenty-five but if my said granddaughter should die without issue, then the said Negro girl and the issue if any to be sold for the*

---

[39] Register of Wills for Frederick County, Maryland, *(1783-1794), Nicholas Hall,* Liber HS-2-422, 9 January 1821.

*residue of her and their time of service and the
proceeds of the said sale to be equally divided among
all my following grandchildren, to wit; my two
grandsons John Henry Hall and Nicholas Hall and
the children of my two daughters each of my said
grandchildren to have an equal share.*

Charity's sister, "Negro girl Betty," was similarly dispatched
to another granddaughter, Martha, to serve until being freed
in 1840. Hall's will then goes on to establish dates from
1827 through 1850 for some additional 16 named slaves to be
set free. According to Hall descendant Nick Wood, about
half of the graves in the family cemetery were for the
family's former slaves.

The Halls were by no means the only slave-owners in New
Market. Slaves were sold on Main Street on a regular basis.
Marguerite Burgee recalls that her ancestor Singleton
Burgee, "had 99 slaves and wanted to have 100 but couldn't
make it." However, it was a woman named Rachel Smith
who appears to have the most notorious reputation as a
slaveholder. In her last will and testament, transcribed
hereafter, Rachel seeks to determine the future of her slaves
even after her own demise.[40]

African-Americans represented a significant portion of the
town's population in the mid-1800s even as now. By the
Civil War, the number of freed slaves was increasing. Also,
during the war, many African-American men in New Market
enlisted in the Union Army. Those who had been slaves
became free men by virtue of their military service.

---

[40] Register of Wills for Frederick County, Maryland, (1783-1794), *Rachel Smith,* GME-2,
670-671, 22 March 1842.

Last Will and Testament of Rachel Smith

In the name of God, Amen. I Rachel Smith of Frederick County and State of Maryland, being weak of body, but of sound mind, memory, and understanding, considering the certainty of death and the uncertainty of the time thereof, and being desirous to settle my worldly affairs and thereby be the better prepared to leave this world when it shall please God to call me home, do therefore make and publish this my last Will and Testament, in manner and from the following, that is to say:

First and principally, I commit my soul to the hands of the Almighty God, and my body to the earth to be decently buried at the discretion of my Executor hereinafter named and after my debts are and funeral charges are paid, I devise and bequeath as follows:

Item. I give and devise unto my oldest son John H.M. Smith four hundred dollars, and my Negro girl Louisa, to serve until she shall arrive at the age of thirty-five years; then I devise that she shall be free. I devise further that if the said John H.M. Smith should die before the time of said Negro Louisa's servitude shall expire, then that said Negro girl shall be the property of my grand daughter Mary Hamilton Anderson.

Item. I give and devise unto my daughter Ann Anderson, my Negro woman Minty Ann, to serve until the said Minty Ann shall arrive at the age of thirty-five years, then I devise that she shall be free.

Item I give and bequeath to my daughter Ann Anderson, my saddle, bridle, and all my wearing apparel.

Item. *I give, devise, and bequeath unto my grandson Philemon Smith Anderson, the house and lot situated in New Market, Fred. Co., MD. Together with my Negro boy Isaac to serve until he should arrive at the age of thirty-five years; then I devise that he shall be free. Further I give and bequest to him the said Philemon Smith Anderson one-half dozen chairs, one cupboard, and my* (word un-deciphered) *feather bed and bedding, also one sow & goat and my square red table.*

Item. *I give, devise, and bequeath unto my grandson Thomas Anderson son of my daughter Ann Anderson my house and lot lying near the B &O R. Road* (sic) *in Frederick County, which was deeded to me by Tyer Wright: Also I give and bequest to him the said Thomas Anderson one bow, and one bed & bedding and my large dining table.*

Item. *I give, devise, and bequest unto my grandson William P. Anderson, son of my daughter Ann Anderson, my Negro boy Abraham, to serve until he shall arrive at the age of thirty-five years; then I devise that he shall be free; also I give and bequest unto the said Wm. P. Anderson my Negro boy Noah, to serve until he shall arrive at the age of thirty-five years; then I devise that he shall be free. In reference to this last boy Noah, I devise that he shall not be taken from his mother under three years of age.*

Item. *I give, devise, and bequeath unto my grandson Henry Mortimer Anderson, son of my daughter Ann Anderson, my Negro boy George to serve until he shall arrive at the age of thirty-five years; then I devise that he shall be free. I also give and bequest unto the said Henry Mortimer*

Anderson my large looking glass, one clock, and one small table and one bed and bedding.

Item. I give, bequeath, and devise unto my grand daughter Mary Hamilton Smith Anderson, child of my daughter Ann Anderson, my Negro girl Miranda to serve until she shall arrive at the age of thirty-five years; then I devise that she shall be free. I also give unto said Mary Hamilton Smith Anderson one bureau and lookglass (sic) and small tables.

Item. I give and bequeath unto my son Philemon M. Smith fifty dollars.

Item. I give and bequest that all the residue of my effects, consisting various articles of household & kitchen furniture shall be equally divided between my children Ann Anderson, John H.M. Smith and my grandson Philemon Smith Anderson.

And lastly, I do hereby constitute and appoint my grandson William Pinkney Anderson Executor of this my last Will and Testament revoking and annulling all former wills by me made heretofore, certifying this and none other to be my last will and testament. In testimony whereof, I have hereunto set my hand and affixed my seal this third day of September, Eighteen hundred & forty-one.

X (Mark of Rachel Smith)

Note: When a copy of this will was transcribed from the original files in Annapolis, Maryland, the transcriber mistakenly identified the mark as that of "Raphael Smith" even though her name in the first line of the document is written clearly as "Rachel Smith." Unfortunately, mistakes of this sort are not uncommon.

In his 1977 family history (described in Chapter 11), Dr. H. Hanford Hopkins IV identifies another woman in the local area who was a large slaveholder in the early 1800s: Cordelia Dorsey, widow of William Downey, Sr., and daughter of Basil Dorsey, Jr., who owned "Dorsey's Search," a large plantation just north of New Market. Ultimately, Cordelia inherited the almost-1900-acre plantation along with 420 acres on either side of the county road (Route 874) north from New Market to New London. According to Hopkins, Cordelia owned some eighty-five slaves, had an overseer, but managed the farming herself.

Union Re-enactors.

CHAPTER 9

The Civil War Days

When Nicholas Hall and William Plummer surveyed and sold lots for what would become the Town of New Market in the early 1790s, they had no idea that, only seventy years later, their town would find itself situated within forty miles (as the crow flies) of six major battles in the War Between the States:

- First Battle of Bull Run at Manassas, Virginia, forty miles south of New Market, on 21 July 1861;
- Second Battle of Bull Run, at the same location, on 29-30 August 1862;
- Battle of South Mountain, Maryland, approximately twenty miles west of New Market, on 14 September 1862;
- Battle of Antietam at Sharpsburg, Maryland, twenty-seven miles west of New Market, on 16-17 September 1862;
- Battle of Gettysburg, Pennsylvania, thirty-four miles north of New Market, on 1-3 July 1863;
- Battle of the Monocacy, near Frederick, Maryland, only seven miles west of New Market, on 9 July 1864.

Nor was the City of Frederick ignored.

In July 1864, Federal forces abandoned it, and Confederate troops under the command of Lt. General Jubal Early

New Market
Roads to Gettysburg

GETTYSBURG CAMPAIGN

Late in June 1863, the Union Army of the Potomac pursued Gen.
Robert E. Lee's Army of Northern Virginia as it invaded the North less
than a year after the Antietam Campaign. On Monday, June 29, the
Federal corps marched north toward Pennsylvania on parallel roads like
the fingers of a glove, after being ordered to stay between Lee and the
large Northern cities.

Gen. John F. Reynolds led I Corps west of Frederick on Emmitsburg
Road (present-day U.S. Rte. 15), while General Oliver O. Howard and
XI Corps tramped Old Frederick Road to Emmitsburg. Commanding
General George G. Meade, with III and XII Corps and the artillery
reserve, moved on what is now Rte. 194. Gen. Winfield Scott
Hancock's II Corps and Meade's V Corps (soon placed under Gen.
George Sykes) marched northeastward along present-day Rt. 26 to
Liberty and Unionville. Gen. John Sedgwick's VI Corps, which
guarded the army's right flank, moved by here to Mount Airy and
Westminster, reaching Manchester on June 30. The next day, the corps
began an epic 34-mile march to Gettysburg and arrived late in the
afternoon of July 2.

A soldier in the 37th Massachusetts Infantry, VI Corps, later wrote that
on entering New Market, "two or three young ladies were discovered
standing in front of their home waving small Union flags. It was an
electrifying sight, and the enthusiasm which had pervaded the troops in
advance was emphasized from the strong throats of the Thirty-seventh.
There was no question now that they were in the land of friends."

The above transcribes Civil War activity in the New Market/Monrovia from a
Maryland Civil War Trails marker at the Messanelle Memorial Park near 21 W.
Main Street in New Market. The sign also displays oval portraits of Gen. George
Meade, Gen. John Reynolds, Gen. Oliver Howard, Gen. Winfield Hancock, Gen.
George Sykes, and Gen. John Sedgwick, along with a map of the area.

June 29 midday 1863
VI Corps in New Market/Monrovia

New union commander George G. Meade orders his army north with two objectives: Engage the Confederate Army under the best possible conditions while protecting Washington, D.C.

Learning that the Union army was close and getting closer, Lee orders his army to consolidate somewhere near the Maryland-Pennsylvania border.

occupied it, demanding a ransom of $200,000 or the city would be burned.[41] The ransom was paid.

The Town of New Market and nearby Village of Monrovia had some significance during the Civil War if only because of their locations along the Baltimore Pike and B&O Railroad. At various times during the war, Union or Confederate forces occupied this area. For example:

- Brig. General Fitzhugh Lee's Confederate brigade "sat astride the Baltimore and Ohio Railroad in and around New Market in September 1862."
- Also in 1862, Confederate General J.E.B. Stuart made his headquarters for a time at the Landon House in Urbana, only seven miles southwest of New Market, after the Army of Northern Virginia invaded Maryland. According to a marker currently at the site, the building was constructed in 1754 on the banks of the Rappahannock River in Virginia. It was reconstructed at its present site in 1846 and became the "Landon Female Academy." The Landon House was the scene of the historic "Sabers and Roses Ball" hosted by Stuart on 7 September 1862 to welcome the Confederate cavalry who had just arrived in town. Ladies in the local area

[41] Daniel Carroll Toomey, *The Civil War in Maryland,* Toomey Press, Baltimore, 6th ed., 1993, 47, 105-109, 118-120.

attended, and the regimental band of the 18th Mississippi Cavalry provided the music. At various times during the war, the Landon House accommodated injured personnel from both sides. For example, it served as a place to treat wounded Union soldiers following the Battle of South Mountain. The Landon House still stands proudly at 3401 Urbana Pike and currently accommodates weddings, tours, and special events in keeping with its historic significance.

- In July 1864, Lt. Colonel D.R. Clendenin withdrew his Eighth Illinois Cavalry forces to Monrovia where he found wagons loaded with wounded soldiers and infantry making their way east after the Battle of the Monocacy.

Nick Wood notes that New Market maintained its own home guard during the Civil War. Nick relates this folk story told about the home guard:

> *When Jeb Stuart came through here on his way to Gettysburg, they (i.e., members of the New Market home guard) buried their weapons under an outhouse behind the Hopkins house so the Confederates wouldn't get them. Jeb Stuart was delayed at Westminster, Maryland, and didn't get to Gettysburg on time.*

Confederate Re-enactors, c. 1993, courtesy of Shirley Shaw.

The Battle of the Monocacy in July 1864 was the Civil War battle closest to New Market and Monrovia and also is known as "The Battle that Saved Washington."[42] Lt. General Jubal Early's Confederates defeated the Union forces led by Major General Lew Wallace, but the battle sufficiently delayed the Confederates until Union reinforcements could be assembled for the defense of the nation's capital. After-action reports written by several Union officers include these excerpts concerning activities in the New Market area:

> *...Our wounded left on the field were carefully gathered upon the 10th and 11th instant, placed in the general hospital at Frederick, and comfortably provided for. The number in hospital on the 12th when I left that city and when, I believe, every man had been taken from the field, was 189. To these should be added 15 cases which I found at New*

[42] B. Franklin Cooling, *Monocacy: The Battle That Saved Washington,* White Mane Publishing Co., Inc., Shippensburg, Pa., 1997, 157-158, 171-173.

Campfire Cooking
Re-enactment

Market, several miles this side of Frederick, making a total of 204... (From 14 July 1864 report by G. K. Johnson, Medical Inspector, U.S. Army.)

...The men now learned from citizens that the main body of the army had moved out some two hours before, and this, with the increasing fire of the enemy on my flank, produced considerable confusion, during which the men broke and threw away their guns and accouterments (sic) and attempted to save themselves. This information received and that they were surrounded and would be made prisoners, caused them to break their guns to prevent them falling into the enemy's hands. I succeeded, however, in bringing off about 300 of my command, with which I joined the main body at New Market about 8 p.m... (From 14 July 1864 report by Col. Allison L. Brown, commander of the 149th Regiment, Ohio National Guard.)

...At 12 o'clock at night I arrived on the Baltimore pike, two miles this side of New Market, and found that the enemy had not been on the road farther than New Market. I brought up the rear guard with eight men to one mile on the other side of Ridgeville, (i.e.,

*in present-day Mt. Airy) and there met my command,
I reported to Lieutenant-Colonel Clendenin for
orders...(From 18 July 1864 report by Captain
Edward H. Leib, Fifth U.S. Cavalry, commanding
Mounted Infantry.)*

*...We moved out along the road at a walk, which led
to the Baltimore pike, and I was ordered by General
Wallace, at New Market, to proceed along the road to
Baltimore. Two of the guns were left in the rear to
assist in guarding the column, though with little
ammunition left, and joined the battery at Ellicott's
Mills at 11 a.m. Sunday, July 10, when I moved to
Baltimore, as ordered, for ammunition and
supplies...(From 13 July 1864 report by Captain
Frederick W. Alexander, commanding Baltimore
Battery of Light Artillery.)*

Subsequently, Sergeant William H. James of the 11th
Maryland, who had gone home to Baltimore on 11 July 1864,
returned with portions of his regiment to picket in the New
Market-Monrovia-Mt. Airy area.

There is little specific information about other wartime
activities in Monrovia, although Civil War souvenirs found
on the farms there indicate skirmishes. The New York
Herald of 16 September 1862 reportedly carried a front-page
article concerning the Village of Monrovia, Maryland, and its
involvement in the Civil War. Unfortunately, that newspaper
is defunct, and copies of the article no longer can be
obtained. One example of such involvement, however, was
in 1863 when Confederate troops burned the B&O Railroad
siding at Monrovia in an attempt to interfere with Union
troop movements.

Choosing Sides

The people of New Market, like others living so close to the Mason-Dixon Line, were divided in their loyalties during the Civil War. Some joined the Confederacy, while others supported the Union. The local population included Caucasians as well as African-Americans - slaves as well as freed. Those who owned slaves were far less likely to support emancipation. On the other hand, some local citizens went out of their way to show support for union soldiers. In another such case, local residents put containers of drinking water alongside the road in New Market for retreating federal soldiers following the Union defeat at the Monocacy Battlefield.

Confederate cavalry units often rode into Frederick County, not only as a show of strength, but also to recruit local citizens or to obtain food for themselves and fodder for their horses. The New Market/Monrovia area was among the local communities reached on these incursions.

CHAPTER 10

Local Churches

Churches in New Market are few in number but long in history. There have been as many as five churches at one time during its more than 200 years, but only three remain within the town today.

Grace Episcopal Church

On East Main Street, Grace Episcopal Church began as a mission in May 1870. The first rector there was the Reverend James Stephenson, S.T.D., native of Ireland. He also is known for establishing missions in Mt. Airy (St. James) and in Poplar Springs (St. Paul's). Collectively, these missions formed the Linganore Parish in the Diocese of Maryland.

The original Grace Church was constructed in 1872,[43] and a nearby house was purchased in 1879 to serve as a rectory for the church. The church was the scene of a serious fire in 1902, causing much interior damage. Only the brick walls were left standing, but the townspeople were able to save the pews by carrying them outside. The people also rescued a memorial tablet dedicated in memory of the church's first rector, but the church had to be rebuilt. After the work was finished, the church reopened in 1903. Two years later, the church bought a new pump organ from the Estey Organ Company of Brattleboro, Vermont, and the current windows were donated in 1909. Electrical service was not provided until 1923. At least two of the old kerosene lamps subsequently were electrified. Through the present day, the old church has had no indoor plumbing.

Renovations to the structure were made in 1954 under the direction of the Reverend Leon P.F. Vauthier, who had been pastor for twenty-one years. The church closed from May until November while repairs were being made. For example, the original kerosene lamps dating to the 1890s had to be replaced with modern electrical illumination. Members of the building committee included the Chairman, Stoll D. Kemp, along with members Mr. and Mrs. Bernard Selby, Mrs. Olive Sponseller, and Lucian Falconer. One improvement involved extending the vestibule upward to a bell tower. This brick tower with its four-foot gold cross on top has become the dominant feature identifying the church as Grace Episcopal. A special ceremony was held to celebrate the reopening of the church, with the Right Reverend Noble C. Powell, then bishop of the Episcopal Diocese of Maryland in Baltimore, officiating.

---

[43] *The News,* Frederick, Md., "Bishop Conducts Reopening Service in New Market Church," November 29, 1954.

Among the rectors who served Grace Episcopal over the years following the Rev. Stephenson, these names are recalled: Rev. Leon Vauthier, from France (1933-1956), Rev. Robert Jacques (1973-1984), and Rev. Columba Dilliss, who was rector for at least ten years, starting in 1990. During periods when no priest resided in New Market, priests from Urbana or Frederick sometimes helped out by conducting services there. At other times, for example from 1966 to 1973, lay-readers George Delaplaine and Walter Kirk saw to it that Sunday services were maintained.

Currently, the Rev. Mary-Patricia Ashby is the Priest in Charge serving the spiritual needs of the Grace Episcopal community, about ninety-five families. Rev. Ashby points out that the congregation has outgrown the old church on Main Street. A new church is being planned. It will be located on the old Archibald Farm at 5740 Green Valley Road, just north of Old New Market Road. Following the death of the farm's owner, Fred Archibald, who also owned a Baltimore newspaper, a parishioner bought the property three years ago and donated it to the church. The farm, now known as the Grace Episcopal Church Farm, comprises some 26 ½ acres and a very large yellow house, which currently is being used by the church for a variety of activities.

Rev. Ashby says that the church has been working with an architect on a master plan, which recently was presented to the congregation. The design calls for a transitional facility to be built first and, later, a new and larger church. The transitional building will be used for Sunday school and for the family service on Sundays. She notes, however, "We will continue to use the church in town for early services."

New Market United Methodist Church

In 1801, a log building, or meeting house, was erected on North Alley in New Market to serve as the town's first Methodist church.[44,45] Its founder and first minister, Rev. James L. Higgins later became the first ordained bishop of the Methodist Church in the United States. In 1821, a two-story brick church was built on the same site as the log building. During renovations in 1957 when the church's floor was changed, workers discovered the stone foundation of the original log building underneath the old flooring.

The church's brick exterior is typified by its traditional simplicity. It was built, however, with some unusual features - such as its two separate entrances, one for ladies and one for gentlemen, so that they could be seated on opposite sides of the church. The windows on both sides of the church, closest to the front doors, originally were doors that led up to a "slave gallery" - a balcony used to accommodate slaves during the prayer services.

This church has had more than 100 pastors and assistants during its years in New Market. Most served for only a few years. The exception was the Reverend K.D. Swecker, who

[44] New Market United Methodist Church Directory, *History,* circa 1969 (undated).
[45] *Folger McKinsey, "Methodism Has Long History in New Market Community", The Sun,* Baltimore, September 24, 1941.

served from 1940 to 1949. The current pastor of New Market UMC is Rev. Dennis Upton. Originally, the church was called the Methodist Episcopal Church, but it was renamed the New Market Methodist Church following the 1939 union of the American Methodists. Later, following the national unification of the Methodist and the Evangelical United Brethren Church, the church adopted its current name, the New Market United Methodist Church.

There are two cemeteries associated with the church. The older burial ground, the Methodist Episcopal Cemetery, contains the graves of many of the original settlers of New Market with such names as: Anderson, Baldwin, Brown, Falconer, Adamson, Barbour, Bayer, Howard, Griffith, Delaplanch, Burgess, Mount, Buckingham, Scott, Solomon, Stephens, Nelson, Ervin, Greentree, Wood, Wright, and Hanna. Gravestones in the newer cemetery nearby indicate such common New Market names as Bussard, Dorsey, Zimmerman, Boyer, Downey, Shaw, Hammond, Talbott, Hyatt, Mealey, Dronenberg, and many others.

The Zimmermans are worthy of special mention here. Paul Zimmerman, Sr., recorded an audiotape detailing some of the history of the New Market United Methodist Church before he passed away in 1992. He left the tape in the hands of his son,

Stone Marking the Grave of Early New Market Settler Benjamin Wright (1790-1827).

Paul, Jr., who still lives in New Market. In the recording, Paul, Sr., indicates that his account was based on information handed down from four generations of his family living in New Market, starting with his mother's grandfather, Thomas Etcheson, who was born there in 1817.

The New Market UMC is said to be the second oldest practicing Methodist church in Maryland – second only to one in Baltimore.

Various Methodist Churches Over Time in New Market

c. 1801 – **Log Meeting House** erected at the same site as the current United Methodist Church. It provided shelter from wind, rain, and snow. Candles or lard oil lamps provided light.

1821 – Two-story brick structure replaced the log building and became known as the **Methodist Episcopal Church**. The Rev. John Pitts and Rev. James L. Higgins were two of its first pastors.

1831 – **Methodist Protestant Church** was organized, and a church was erected at the east end of town, next to the residence at 1 E. Main Street. Its first pastor was I. Ibbertson. It remained there until Dr. Ernest Roop bought the property in 1941. He removed the church's cemetery and reset its grave markers behind the Methodist Church's educational building. All that remains today of the former church site are the iron fence and gate on Main Street. The parsonage for the Methodist Protestant Church was at the nearby Smith Tavern building from 1855 to 1885, as mentioned in Chapter 3.

1844 – General Conference of 1844 in New York City resulted in two separate branches of American Methodists over the issue of slavery.

1867 – Post-Civil War schism over slavery ultimately results in the New Market congregation becoming divided and a separate Methodist Episcopal Church South being established in a building just to the left of 60 W. Main Street. Its first pastor was J.P. Hall. Not rebuilt after being destroyed by fire in 1918.

1918 – **Methodist Episcopal Church South** destroyed in fire and never rebuilt.

1939 – As a result of the Union of American Methodists, the former **New Market Methodist Episcopal Church** became known as **New Market Methodist Church**.

1940 – **Methodist Protestant Church** became united with **Methodist Episcopal Church**. Former **Methodist Protestant Church** building razed in 1941.

Subsequently, with the national unification of Methodists with the Evangelical United Brethren Church, the New Market church assumed its current name: **New Market United Methodist Church (UMC)**.

The New Market Fire of 1918[46]

On the night of 17-18 March 1918, fire began to spread through a number of buildings in town, including the Methodist Episcopal Church South, the residences of Charles Utz, Isabel Dorsey, and Theodore Stevens as well as Stevens' garage, meat house, and blacksmith shop. Much of the town was at risk. County Commissioner Harry Wood first spotted the fire about 10:30 p.m. He happened to be returning home along with his sister, Jennie Wood. He quickly alerted occupants of the burning buildings as well as other residents. Some of them formed bucket brigades to fight the rapidly spreading fire while many others carried furniture out of their homes to prevent it from being destroyed. Their efforts fairly succeeded in that the fire was just about under control by the time that equipment arrived from the Independent Hose Company located in Frederick.

[46] *The News,* Frederick, Md., "New Market Fire Damage near $10,000," March 18, 1918.

Simpson Christian Community Church

Located at 24 E. Main Street, this nondenominational church was built to replace an earlier church built in 1859 on North Alley, next to the Simpson Cemetery. The former Bethel AME (Afro-American Methodist Episcopal) Church was built of logs and had a balcony.

Reverend Pastor R.H. Jackson oversaw construction of the new place of worship on E. Main Street until its completion in 1948. It has since become non-denominational. The Simpson Christian Community Church is of wood frame construction, with a bell tower, and is painted white. The current pastor is J. Sherman Mason, Jr.

CHAPTER 11

Some Glimpses of Town Life
In the 1800s and 1900s

Pictures may tell better than words what life was like in New Market years ago. This chapter, therefore, includes old photographs which have been treasured and saved over the years and have been made available for use in this book. First, however, something must be said about key professionals who contributed so much on behalf of the early citizens of New Market.

Pioneers of Medicine

For much of its history, New Market has been known for its fine doctors, starting with Dr. Belt Brashear, who was born in Frederick County in 1770. After studying medicine, possibly in Philadelphia, he established his practice in New Market during its early years. Dr. Brashear died in 1834.

Other notable local physicians included Dr. Jesse Wright Downey, who was born in New Market and earned his medical degree from the University of Maryland in 1869; his son, Dr. J.W. Downey, Jr., who was born in New Market, graduated from the University of Virginia in 1905, and practiced in Baltimore; and Dr. Harry W. Dorsey, who was born in New Market and practiced there. Then there was Dr. H. Hanford Hopkins, who was born in Baltimore County,

NEW MARKET
BUSINESS DIRECTORY.

Dry Goods, &c.

Hamilton Stier, Settled 1814, three lots front and five back, Dealer in Dry Goods and Gen'l Merchandise. Adam Boyer, Settled 1869, lots Nos. 35 and 7, Dealer in Dry Goods, Groceries, Hardware, &c.

Physicians.

J. W. Downey, M. D., Settled 1848, Physician and Surgeon.

E. W. Mobberley, M. D., Settled 1824, 492 Acres, Physician and Surgeon.

H. W. Dorsey, M. D., Settled 1866, 273 Acres, Physician and Surgeon.

Hotel.

E. L. Hilton, Settled 1835, 12 Acres, Hilton's Hotel.

Saddle and Harness Maker.

J. T. Lowe, Settled 1865, lot No. 46, Harness and Saddle Manufacturer in general.

Teacher.

Daniel Gibbon, Settled 1872, lot No. 30, Teacher and Minister of the Gospel.

Wagon Maker.

Elias Mount & Son, Settled 1827, Wagon Making in general.

Blacksmith.

David Stephen, Settled 1854, lot 24, Blacksmith in all branches.

Carpenter and Undertaker.

Thomas W. Lease, Settled 1854, lot 28, Carpenter and Undertaker.

Residents.

Chas. Randle, Settled 1872, 190 Acres, W. C. O. R. H. P. Stock Raiser.

John C. Stevens, Settled 1832, lot No. 9, Miller.

N. W. Hammond, Settled 1856, 168 Acres, Retired Merchant.

William W. Ogborn, Settled 1827, 256 Acres, W. C. O. R. H. P. Stock Raiser.

A town plan in the 1873 Titus Atlas of Frederick County identifies three physicians residing and practicing in New Market at that time: Dr. J.W. Downey, Dr. H.W. Dorsey, and Dr. E.W. Mobberley – all physicians and surgeons on Main Street. Additionally, Mobberley's son, Dr. F. W. Mobberley, had his office on South Alley.

Andrew J. Zimmerman (With his Dog "Toby") at New Market's First Gasoline Pump in Front of His Store. Utz Family Photo, c. 1915, Courtesy of Bud Rossig.

married the sister of Dr. J.W. Downey, and then established his own practice in New Market in 1869. Isaac N. Wood was another local physician. These were rather primitive times for the practice of medicine. There were no miracle drugs and no sonograms, CAT scans, or X-ray machines. These men did the best they could – whether it meant setting broken bones, treating bullet wounds, delivering babies, or attempting to cure all manner of illnesses.

In several other cases, these early doctors had sons who became doctors and carried on the profession in New Market for many years. The most striking example involved the Hopkins family with its four generations of physicians by the same name: Howard Hanford Hopkins I, II, III, and IV. The second and third of these were town physicians in New Market.[45]

---

[45] H. Hanford Hopkins IV, *Captain John Hopkins, Mariner of Philadelphia, and Bideford, in Devon, and His Alleged Forebears and Descendents,* Baltimore, 1977.

Dr. H. H. Hopkins I, the son of John R. Hopkins and Catherine Withers, was born in Lancaster County, Pennsylvania, in 1814. He received his MD from Jefferson Medical College in Philadelphia in 1837 at the age of twenty-three and later moved to Baltimore, where he established his office in 1844. He died of tuberculosis only six years later at the age of thirty-six.

The second Dr. Hopkins, born in 1848, was only two years old when his father passed away. He earned his medical degree at the University of Maryland in 1869, at the very young age of twenty-one. Dr. Hopkins II met his wife-to-be, Margaret Downey, at the summer boarding house of the Morsell Family close to the Monrovia Railroad Station, near New Market. After marrying in 1869, they lived in Baltimore County for a time but then returned to New Market in 1875. They converted a double brick house there to a home and office where he established his medical

Mrs. H. Hopkins II (Marie), 1885 Hopkins Photo, Courtesy of Bud Rossig

practice in New Market, and where he was in competition with his own brother-in-law Dr. Jesse W. Downey.

Dr. Hopkins II was among the first of his profession to recognize the special benefits of sunlight and fresh air. In fact, he built a special cupola in the attic of his home (across the street from what is now Mealey's Restaurant) for his patients to use. They could sit up there, relax, and perhaps read a book while basking in the sun and breathing the fresh air from an open window. Some no doubt enjoyed watching people and their activities down below. Dr. Hopkins also was noted for his treatment of burns. He was gifted in many ways. He loved music, was leader of the New Market Band, and schooled his children in music. His other love was photography. His black and white photographs from the 1880s and 1890s tell much about life in New Market back then. Unfortunately in 1906, the second Dr. Hopkins, like his father, died of tuberculosis at the age of 58.

Dr. H. Hanford Hopkins III was born in 1875 and was raised in New Market. He also graduated from the University of Maryland Medical School, where he received his doctorate in 1895, at the remarkable age of 20. He followed in his father's footsteps to serve the medical needs of the townspeople of New Market.

The Scourge of 1918

Many millions of people died throughout the world, with well over 500,000 in our nation alone. Yes, World War I had been going on for some four years, but that did not cause this disaster. It was the dreaded infectious disease of influenza - causing fever, muscular pains, and inflammation of the respiratory tract.

Highly contagious, this "flu" or "grippe," as it was called, struck the residents of New Market at a time when Dr. H. H. Hopkins III was the town physician. They were fortunate to have him. His professional skills were well respected, and he was particularly noted for his untiring service and devotion to his patients. When the flu hit New Market in 1918, he responded with all the skills and endeavor he could muster. It was not a question of "Is the doctor in?" If someone needed him, day or night, Dr. Hopkins would be there.

Ultimately, this fine doctor himself succumbed to influenza and died on 16 October 1918. Hearing of his death, the people of New Market reportedly gathered to show their respect in front of the doctor's home on Main Street, "perhaps the saddest day in New Market's history."

Dr. Hopkins IV was born in New Market in 1902, and graduated from Johns Hopkins University Medical School in 1927. He married Susan McDermid of Charleston, South Carolina, that same year, and established his medical practice in Baltimore. A noted dermatologist, he served at various times as president of the Baltimore-Washington Dermatology Society and the Baltimore City Medical Society.

Obviously, a New Market boy who made good, H. Hanford Hopkins IV received the Distinguished Alumnus Award from the Johns Hopkins University and School of Medicine in 1972. In his family history of 1977,[46] he indicates that his son and grandson were named Howard Hanford Hopkins V and VI, respectively, but he makes no mention of either following the family medical tradition. In tracing his family origins, he found that his forefathers had come from Devon,

[46] Ibid

England, by way of Philadelphia and Bairdford, Pennsylvania, before coming to Maryland.

Riggs Sanitarium

Another noteworthy local physician was Dr. George Henry Riggs (1870-1957). He was well known and was very highly regarded for his treatment of mental patients and for his establishment of the Riggs Sanitarium in nearby Ijamsville, Maryland, in 1896. Dr. Riggs was considered to be one of the leading psychiatrists of his time in Maryland, reportedly caring for more than 1,000 patients from throughout the nation. Remarkably, he somehow found time to maintain his own private medical practice in Ijamsville. A former patient of his recalled that Dr. Riggs would charge one or two dollars for making house calls in those days.

The local restaurant known for many years as "Gabriel's Inn" on Ijamsville Road previously housed the Riggs Sanitarium.

Hopkins' Photographs

Following are several pages of photographs by Dr. Hopkins II. The pictures are from various dates between 1885 and 1900, long before the days of sophisticated cameras or high-resolution color films. Clothing too was quite different then. Men's hats, for example, ranged from the broad-brimmed western-style to the more formal derby hats or "bowlers." Straw hats were fashionable for men during the summertime. Also apparent in the old photographs are the high-collar shirts and characteristic ties that men wore, along with a vest and coat. Beards and mustaches were fairly common. Women of the day can be seen with their full-length skirts and dresses, white blouses, conservative hairstyles, and flat-brimmed hats.

New Market Hotel Proprietor Philimon Howard Griffith and Daughter. Hopkins Photo, Courtesy of Bud Rossig.

Townfolks Gather at William Downey Home. Hopkins Photo, c. 1895, Courtesy of Bud Rossig.

New Market Band of 1890. Hopkins Photo, Courtesy of Bud Rossig.

Horse and Handler on Main Street in Late 1800s. Hopkins Photo, Courtesy of Bud Rossig.

Model T Ford on Main Street. Utz Family Photo (c. 1915-1918), Courtesy of
Bud Rossig.

Formal Group Portrait, 1892 Hopkins photo, Courtesy of Bud Rossig.

Watermelon Feast, 1899 Hopkins Photo, Courtesy of Bud Rossig.

Main Street in Late 1800s. Hopkins Photo, Courtesy of Bud Rossig.

The pictures showing simple, informal gatherings – as well as the one group portrait – suggest that these were a people who were comfortable and at peace with each other. The "New Market Roosters" even had a jokester in their group, it seems.

"New Market Roosters:" Frank Downey, Percy Russell, Dr. H. Hanford Hopkins, and John Detrick. Hopkins Photo, Courtesy of Bud Rossig.

The simple, plain view of Main Street - devoid of cars and trucks - seems so peaceful and pleasant. There are a few examples of the mode of transportation of the day: a riding horse, horse and carriage, horse and sleigh in the winter, a bicycle, and even a unicycle. And, "man's best friend" stands posted in front of the hotel as the world passes by.

Grandson's Recollections as a Youth

Hopkins' grandson, H. Hanford Hopkins IV, in his family history, shared these memories of his youthful years in New Market:

One of my childhood pleasures was to watch Hantz Jackson, the blacksmith, shoe horses and build beautiful four-horse wagons from the raw wood and iron. I also watched antique furniture restored and refinished in the machine shop, but the greatest delight was to sneak off to the village pool room, a forbidden place of sin, according to my mother, and learn to play pocket billiards. I worked one whole summer in the carriage factory, for 25 cents a day. My job was to cut and sew up side curtains for buggies. I also thinned corn for farmers, a back-breaking job.

(See "Thinning Corn" below for a description of that activity.)

Charlotte Houser Remembers Growing Up in the Early 1900s

Lucien Falconer, who was born and raised in New Market and now lives in Frederick, invited me to accompany him on a visit to his ninety-seven-year-old aunt, Charlotte Houser, on 5 April 2004. Charlotte currently lives in the Charlestown Retirement Community in Catonsville, Maryland. She too was born and raised in New Market and has fond memories of the town.   – JFS

It was 1906 when Charlotte Falconer came into this world. Almost a century later, her hearing is not as good as she would like, and she has to use a wheel chair. But this fine lady recalls events about which many of us have only heard or read. She was almost eight years old, for example, when Archduke Francis Ferdinand of Austria was assassinated and World War I began in 1914. She was twenty-three at the time of the New York Stock Exchange Crash of 1929 and

Charlotte (Falconer) Houser in 2004.

knew the full impact of the Great Depression days of the 1930s. Charlotte left New Market in the mid-1930s and married William Houser, who was an engineer at the Capitol Power Plant. They lived in Lanham, Maryland.

Charlotte talked about "the good times playing together" with other youngsters during her childhood days in New Market. "Everybody sat on their front porches" and talked with neighbors walking by. "Everybody knew everybody," she recalled.

The New Market Elementary School in those days had only four rooms. Charlotte remembers her days there, indicating that there were "two rooms down and two rooms up." She also recalls that there were just three stores in town in those days, and the Stevens Family had a business making buggies on W. Main Street, along with a blacksmith shop. The business changed with the times and later became an auto repair shop, according to Charlotte's nephew, Lucien Falconer.

"During World War I, we used to make wash cloths – crocheted or knitted them – for our troops," Charlotte noted. As for the Great Depression, she said, "There were lots of things we had to go without and couldn't have." She found that much the same was true during World War II, when many needed items had to be rationed. In talking about hard times such as these, or even her present circumstances, Charlotte does not complain but seems to gather strength and satisfaction from her experiences over time. When interviewed for this book, she was looking forward to celebrating her 98th birthday on 6 November 2004.

Canning Beans and Corn in the 1930s

As mentioned in Chapter 7, a cannery was situated along the railroad tracks in Monrovia, just a few blocks from New Market. The business employed many people from the immediate area and elsewhere during the harvest season because, in the 1930s, the work had to be done by hand. Betty Jeffers still lives in Monrovia, and she remembers those days very well:

> *In the mid-thirties, green beans and corn were canned there. The beans were snipped and cut by hand. My father (Leslie Davis) worked for George W. McComus (who owned the cannery), and everyone in my family – mother, two sisters, and myself – worked in the factory at one time or other. At the busiest of times, my father would bring home wooden crates of beans so that we could help snip them.*

There also were migrant workers who would come down from Pennsylvania to work at the cannery during the canning season. Looking back to those times, Betty adds: "I can remember it being a big day in town when they arrived."

"Trucking in the Twenties" – and Beyond

H. Bernard Selby was an ambitious young man in the 1920s. He lived in New Market, he owned his own truck, and he put it to work to make a living for his family. He hauled milk from local farmers to area dairies from 1920 to 1954, according to his son Howard. In the late 1930s, Selby expanded his commercial trucking business, hauling lumber from four or five local sawmills to points throughout the area, wherever it was needed. For example, he brought loads of lumber all the way to Point-of-Rocks Bridge on the Potomac River so that new concrete forms could be built to replace flood-damaged support columns.

Bernard Selby's hard work and success as a businessman seems to have paid off well. In 1940, he was elected Mayor of New Market and held that post until 1949, when Franklin Smith replaced him. Mayor Selby died in 1956.

Growing Up in the 1930s and 1940s

June Snowden has lived long enough in New Market to remember what life was like in the early 1940s. She remembers hearing the news that the Japanese attacked Pearl Harbor on 7 December 1941 as if it were yesterday. June also remembers that, just after World War II, when she and her friends were ten to twelve years old, they had some work to do. "We picked beans for Dick Mealey's hotel," she recalls. June smiles as she tells how she and many other children in town would be picked up and taken to the Mealey farm in nearby Monrovia, where "acres and acres of string beans" had been planted. It was a chance for the youngsters to earn some spending money.

Harvested beans were taken to the Monrovia Cannery as in the 1930s. When she got older, June found employment there. Most of all, however, she remembers picking beans for the hotel. "Miss Sarah Pryor was the cook then," June recalls, noting that Miss Sarah was head of the kitchen, canned the beans, and made corn relish as well as other tasty things that a child would remember well.

Ms. Snowden has other fond memories of her childhood, growing up in her family's small log home at 15 East Main Street (further described in Chapter 15). She remembers several of the town's early doctors, and especially their wives, who were so kind to her and from whom she learned so much. Dr. Ernest Roop, for example, lived just up the street from her at 1 East Main Street. The building had two doors, one for his residence, and the other for his office. Dr. Roop delivered June when she was born as well as some of her siblings. As a child, June often did chores for some of the doctors' wives, such as sweeping floors or going on errands. In particular, she remembers Mrs. Jane Downey and Mrs. Maggie Hopkins. "I learned a lot from those ladies," she says. Now June realizes that what they taught her was more valuable than the fifty cents she might have been given.

Dr. Roop operated his family practice in town until the 1950s and, along with Dr. Ralph Michel, was one of the last practicing physicians in New Market. Each of the local towns seemed to have its own physician living and practicing in the town. Dr. Roop's son Donald also became a doctor. Sadly, Dr. Ernest Roop was killed in an auto accident. Marguerite Burgee and others in New Market recall the tragic incident. She notes that Donald had been following his father in his own car "to make sure he got home all right," and witnessed the tragedy. On a lighter note, Marguerite relates how the senior Dr. Roop seemed to be a bit absent-minded:

> *He would sometimes forget his hat when leaving after a house call, or he would go through the wrong door going down to the cellar.*

By all accounts, however, Dr. Roop was very well liked.

"Thinning Corn"

Howard B. Selby, previously mentioned son of former Mayor Selby, recalls his childhood days growing up in New Market in the 1930s and early 1940s. His family lived in a house on Main Street across from the elementary school. Just as June Snowden recalls picking beans to earn spending money as a youngster, Howard looks back on how he and his friends made seventy-five cents per day by "thinning corn" for local farmers. It seems that, when the farmers would plant their corn, sometimes as many as five seeds would fall at a time instead of the desired three seeds. To avoid overcrowding of the cornstalks, they would hire youngsters to pick up two of the five seeds in such cases and replant them. Howard explains that he and his fellow workers would use a long stick fitted with a nail on the end to accomplish this chore. He found that the work was hard on his back, but it put change in his pocket at a time when our nation was still recovering from the Great Depression.

Marguerite Burgee is another person who clearly recollects this practice of thinning corn. She grew up - and still resides - on the 126-acre family farm on Green Valley Road that her father bought in 1905 for $5,000.

Paul Zimmerman, Jr., well remembers those years. His current home at 126 West Main Street sits right on the land that once was his father's cornfield. When ripe, the corn went to the nearby cannery in Monrovia, known as "George W. McComas & Co." Paul Zimmerman, Sr., eventually bought the business from McComas. The corn was canned and sold under several different labels, but, according to Paul, Jr., it was the same corn.

Paul notes that Franklin Smith and Monroe Free also had farms in the area. "Monroe had a basketball net in his barn," Paul recalls, saying that it was a place where farmhands and townspeople would come for some fun and exercise. Hans Jackson, Paul's great-uncle, owned a blacksmith shop just west of the General Store on Main Street, and folks "hung around the blacksmith shop too," according to Zimmerman. Ruth Metz also remembers watching Hans making horseshoes. She laments the fact that "the shop was torn down just before we moved there in 1942."

Paul remembers that German prisoners of war held in nearby Frederick during World War II were often put to work in the cornfields of New Market, guarded by American soldiers. Paul says that they seemed to like the opportunity. Some slipped him notes indicating that they wished to stay here. On one well-remembered occasion, the farm tractor broke down, and work came to a halt. It seems that there was a failure with its magneto, and the engine would not start. One of the prisoners took a look at it and said, "I fix." He was able to fix it because, before the war, he had worked in the German factory where it had been made.

Hits, Strikes, and Balls

Lucien Falconer highlights local baseball games as uppermost in his memories of the 1940s and early 1950s in New Market and neighboring communities. He recalls many Sunday afternoons playing or watching local baseball games. This was not "Little League" baseball, and the players were adult males, not youngsters. New Market's team played in the Maryland State League along with other teams in the area. The New Market club was the hub of the local league and played on its baseball diamond behind the elementary school. The competition generated in this amateur league was outmatched only by the enthusiasm of players and fans alike.

Howard Selby is another former player/fan of those old days of local baseball. After graduating from Frederick High School in 1947, Howard played baseball with the New Market club until one day when he was struck in the face by a ball, which injured his eye and broke his nose. Only 19 at the time, he had to give up baseball, but he remained a fan of his local team and later played softball as an activity sponsored by the New Market Grange.

"The two best pitchers for the New Market Team were Paul Zimmerman, Jr., and Alfred Mayne," Howard recalls, adding:

> The catcher was William J. "Bill" Wilcom, who lived near Urbana close to Araby Church Road. Then there were the "Burrall Boys," Jesse and William, Charles Watkins, Charles Wood, Sam Carson (also a catcher), Ed "Potato" McClain, Paul Welty, and Knowlton Burgee.

Howard remembers the McCutcheon brothers, Wes, a catcher, and Harvey, a pitcher, both of whom played for the Point-Rocks Team. Harvey later played for the old Washington Senators major league team. Paul Zimmerman, Jr., also remembers many of the local players, including Allan Burgess, Paul Chaney, Max Day, Bucky Miller, and Bob Stockman. Paul's father started playing local baseball in the late 1930s and was one of the New Market Team's first managers, along with Merhl Burgee. According to Paul, Jr., Merhl was crippled as a child and could not play baseball but still loved the game and enjoyed managing the team. Marguerite Burgee, who says she is Merhl's "half-cousin," remembers him "spittin' on his hands" with excitement over baseball.

Merhl died in 1978 at the age of fifty-two. His widow, Mary Anna Burgee, tells more about this remarkable man:

> *His first name actually was Luther, but everyone knew him as Merhl. He was handicapped on his hands. He had no knuckles on his hands, and yet he did the most beautiful drawings. For 35 years, he worked at the Davis Taylor Model Basin* [now the Naval Surface Warfare Center at Carderock, Maryland]. *With a co-worker there, Merhl earned a patent for an invention of theirs.* [Mary Ann did not recall what it was.] *He was a charter member of the New Market Lions Club and also was a member of the Hyattstown Fire Company for 30-some years.*

Mary Anna well remembers Merhl's love of baseball and his close friendship with Judge Charles E. Moylan, who managed the Ijamsville Team. Moylan was an Associate Judge for the Supreme Court of Baltimore City for twenty-four years, but his lifetime diversion was baseball, especially playing baseball, coaching, and managing teams in his beloved village of Ijamsville. Remarkably, he did this over many decades, starting in 1909 when his team went undefeated. Playing in the Maryland State League, along with neighboring New Market, Moylan's team went on to win pennants and playoff titles in the 1930s, 1940s, and 1950s. Paul Zimmerman describes Moylan as more than a mere manager: "He was president, CEO, and coordinator of the Ijamsville Team and managed the system to get the best players for his team." In this regard, there was a restriction limiting teams to recruiting only players who lived within fifteen miles of their home field. Ijamsville's home games were at Moxley Field, close to Bush Creek, where more than one baseball was lost. It is said that scouts from the Baltimore Orioles major league team occasionally showed up there to check out some of the local players. Moxley Field still exists but has been used chiefly by a pony club in recent times.

The local teams scheduled their baseball games early on Sunday afternoons so that the players, many of whom were farmers, could get home in time to milk their cows.

In addition to the New Market and Ijamsville clubs, other teams of the Maryland State League, according to Paul Zimmerman, Jr., included Beallsville, Brunswick, Frederick, Jefferson, Libertytown, Lovettsville, Mt. Airy, Point-of-Rocks, and Thurmont. Not all were members at one time. Paul recalls that they would come in and out of the league at various times in the late 1930s, 1940s, 1950s, and "maybe into the early 1960s." Paul thinks that his father was one of those who started playing ball in New Market in the 1930s, along with a player by the name of Sam Carson and others.

Paul, Jr., recalls 1956 as the year that New Market won the state championship.

Organized amateur baseball was not just a phenomenon local to the New Market area. In addition to the Maryland State League, there was also the Tri-State League, which included teams from Broad Run, Creagerstown, Damascus, Middletown, and Walkersville. Every year the two leagues played an all-star game, just as in the major leagues. Paul adds that there also was a third local league, the "Heart of Maryland League," which accommodated players who were either too young or too old to play in the regular leagues. New Market, Ijamsville, and Taylorsville fielded teams in this league, along with Boliver (in Washington County, Maryland).

Half a century of local baseball in western Maryland should be remembered for the pleasure, excitement, and healthy diversion it provided for players and fans alike, especially coming during a period of great economic depression and several major wars.

From Horses to Cars

Horses and carriages were needed for transportation through much of New Market's history before being replaced by the automobile. Carriage-makers and blacksmiths were much in demand. Several early blacksmith shops were mentioned previously, for example, one at the Smith Tavern and another at 33 West Main St., currently the Victorian Manor.

Paul Zimmerman remembers when blacksmiths still worked in New Market. One example he cites was a blacksmith shop that was located between the General Store and what is now

32 West Main Street. Further west and across the street (i.e., 113 West Main Street), there was another blacksmith shop. It dates back to about 1880 according to Mark Lawson, who, along with his brothers Curtis and Richard, own and run Lawson's Outdoor Power Equipment business at the same site. Mark's great-uncle Richard Lawson founded Lawson's Garage, a car dealership, there in the late 1920s and early 1930s, along with similar dealerships in Ijamsville and Frederick. All were Nash automobile dealerships. Later, Mark's father Richard Lawson took over the business and continued to operate it from the three locations until some major changes came about in the auto industry. As Mark explains it, Nash Motors merged with Hudson and Jeep to form American Motors in the late 1950s. Later, the Chrysler Corporation absorbed all of those manufacturers, and that is when the Lawsons decided to give up the auto dealerships in favor of selling and repairing outdoor power equipment. Some old-timers in New Market, nevertheless, still think of it as "Lawson's Garage."

The Lawson interview was a nostalgic experience for me, since I worked on the assembly line at the Nash Motors auto body plant in Milwaukee, Wisconsin, in 1950-51, during my college years - when the Lawson's were selling these same Nash automobiles approximately 750 miles away in New Market, Maryland. - JFS

Reflecting on the Past Quarter Century

Kenneth Valentino was among many who moved to New Market or its adjacent neighborhoods in the latter part of the twentieth century. Like other relative newcomers, he found it to be a more rural area, and he liked that. In the 1980s, one still could enjoy the local pastoral scenes: acres and acres of open land, proud old dairy barns with horses and cattle grazing in nearby pastures or quenching their thirst in nearby ponds. Beautiful? Yes, but these farm operations are important too, since Frederick County has produced twenty-five percent of the milk supply for Maryland.

Like many other "immigrants" to the county, Valentino also found that it was less expensive to buy a home here, and the taxes were lower than in nearby Montgomery County, for example. He saw Frederick County as more inviting overall. Reflecting on this period, Ken observes:

> *...Frederick County was ranked in the top five dairy-producing counties in the U.S. I don't know about now, but back then, scarcely twenty years ago, it was a very agricultural place.*

Why was this rural environment so appealing to Valentino and others like him? He puts it this way:

> *Much of the population increase of the late 1970s and early 1980s came from people and families similar to me. Many of us were construction or some other trade/blue-collar workers, or people from the sixties era who just wanted to get away from the crowds and lifestyle of the close-in metro areas. We saw it as a place to raise children without the drugs and so forth that had become problems in the metropolitan areas of Washington and Baltimore.*

Ken and his wife Norma moved to their New Market address in April 1979. He recalls having spent those twenty-five years since then "working and raising children." He also observes (as others have):

> *One thing I have learned from most of the old-time residents is that, if you have not lived here for a few generations, you are a newcomer.*

This feeling is interesting when one considers that the founders of New Market and many of its most successful entrepreneurs, notably Samuel and Silas Utz, came from elsewhere.

A Story Often Told

There was a young man who moved into Frederick County from a neighboring county in Maryland many years ago. He remained in Frederick for the rest of his long and very successful life. But, when he died ultimately, in his nineties, his newspaper obituary began, "Although not a native of Frederick, Mr._____ ..."   - JFS

Blue Laws

In colonial days in America, and especially in the New England States, there were strict puritanical laws prohibiting business and certain other activities, such as dancing and sports, on the Sabbath. These were known as "Blue Laws." Some readers will recall that somewhat less rigid versions of these Blue Laws still prevailed in local jurisdictions in Maryland well into the twentieth century. Others may never have heard, or have forgotten, about the days back when Blue Laws were in force in Frederick County.   - JFS

Ken Valentino describes what he remembers about local blue laws:

> *One thing I do remember as being new and different for us was that, in 1979/80 and maybe in 1981/82, there were still "Blue Laws" in the County. Stores, some at least, could open on Sundays. Certainly not*

*liquor stores, hardware stores, retail shops, or most
anything that was not an absolute necessity to life.
Food stores could open. We shopped at the Safeway
in Mt. Airy, which was fairly new at the time. On
Sundays, most of the aisles were closed. That is, the
aisle that contained diapers and baby food was open,
but the one with sodas and chips was closed. One of
those stands that say "Wet Floor" would be at each
end of the aisle, and you couldn't shop in that aisle.
So, if you needed bread or milk, you could get that,
but not charcoal or laundry detergent, or paper
towels and cleaning supplies.*

Ken notes also that, during the same years, businesses in the
City of Frederick closed by 6:00 every night, except for
certain restaurants, and generally were closed to most
shopping on Sundays. He adds, "I, for one, thought it was a
great idea, and it reminded me of when I was very little, and
most everything was closed on Sundays."

With the great influx of people moving into Frederick County
in the late 1970s and early 1980s, however, there was
increased pressure to have stores open on Sundays. Finally,
the County abandoned its Blue Laws.

Christmas in New Market, December 1990. Photo Courtesy of Shirley Shaw.

CHAPTER 12

The New Market Grange

New Market Grange in 2004

The New Market Grange traces its history to 13 January 1920 when it was established through the efforts of Brother James Anthony, who was State Organizer for the Grange at that time. The organization was designated then, and still is known as Grange No. 362. The 37 members held regular meetings in the lodge room of the New Market Odd Fellows Hall. (See discussion of "Masonic Lodge" below.)

The word "grange" originated in England. The term refers to a country house with its various farm buildings usually comprising the dwelling of a yeoman (i.e., gentleman farmer). The "Granger Movement" in the United States goes back to about 1867 during the post-Civil War days. It began as a campaign by the "Patrons of Husbandry" (The Grange), a farmers' organization formed for social and cultural purposes.[49,50] At that time, they were campaigning for state control of the railroads and grain elevators, especially in the North Central States. The first Grange, called "Farmers Union Hall," has been described as an early-day union organized to protect farmers from being treated unfairly by the railroads. Many farmers believed that the railroads had been charging them outrageous amounts to take their goods to market. Another problem for the farmers was that carpetbaggers – northern office-holders in the South during post-Civil War reconstruction days – were buying up farmland for next to nothing. The farmers had no representation in Washington and generally were "dirt-poor." They had to organize if they were to survive.

The Grange started out being a secret society. In the beginning, all were farmers, and all were Masons (members of an international secret society having as its principles brotherliness, charity, and mutual aid; also called "Freemasons"). Members had to know a password to be admitted to meetings. There were seven male founders in 1867 plus one woman, subsequently named an honorary founder. The Grange was a rather advanced organization with respect to women in that they were allowed to vote and to hold office.

Once organized, the New Market Grange's first task was to construct a hall where regular meetings could be held. Members cut the timber themselves and then hauled it to a sawmill and back to the building site in New Market. Most directly involved in building the hall were Brothers Frank N.

---

[49] *Webster's New Universal Unabridged Dictionary,* Simon & Schuster, New York, 2nd ed., 1972.

[50] S. Earl Grigsby and Harold Hoffsomer, *Rural Social Organization in Frederick County, Maryland,* Department of Sociology and Agricultural Experiment Station of the University of Maryland, March 1949, 55-57.

Maynard, Nicholas H. Albaugh, Harry O. Mount, J. Burgess Jones, and Charles E. Walker, but many others participated in the construction. The design for the hall reportedly was patterned after a Catholic hall in nearby Libertytown. The New Market hall was built entirely of yellow pine at a total cost of $4,000, plus donations. This first Grange building was dedicated in 1924, but it was not until 1941 that members were able to burn the mortgage.

During World War II, Grange members devoted their main activities to supporting the war effort. There were waste paper and aluminum drives, blood donations, and other efforts in support of the armed forces. After the war, the Grange became involved principally in community service projects. The hall remained under the original ownership until 1964, when ground was broken for a new hall on New Market's South Alley.

The original Grange building, at 1 South Eighth Alley, subsequently became "The Village Gallery," an arts and craft establishment. Later it became an antique shop. Rita Mueller, who bought the property in 1992, operated the shop along with her business partner, Phil Hartman. Rita tells how she looked around for a place where she could live and have a business together, as was common in her native country, Germany. New Market turned out to be just the right place. Appropriately, she called her shop "Grange Hall Antiques."

Phil Hartman was a psychiatric social worker in the Baltimore area before coming to New Market. Phil remembers going to flea markets there, buying small items, and then selling them, something that he enjoys doing. He focuses his interest on antique sports equipment of all kinds.

He collects such memorabilia at various antique shows, such as a recent antique fishing show in Carlisle, Pennsylvania.

Rita recalls the original graffiti on the boiler room basement walls from the days when children would amuse themselves down there while their parents were in a Grange meeting upstairs. She found writings such as: "Bill loves Mary;" or "Mary loves Joe." "Unfortunately," she laments, "Someone cleaned the boiler room walls."

Grange Hall Antiques was open to the public until closing its doors in 2003.

The New Grange on South Alley

The new hall was dedicated on 10 October 1965. It cost $22,139.74 to build. To offset the expense, Grange members undertook fund-raising activities, such as country butchering,

Holiday Celebration at the New Market Grange.

Grange Members Drive in Holiday Parade.

a variety of contests, and providing a food stand at the county fair. In times past, the Grange Hall was used for regular church services and community meetings of all sorts.[51]

To this day, the Grange remains very active, but not just for farmers. Monthly meetings feature guest speakers on such topics as fire prevention, and social security. Currently, there are about seventy members, and the organization reportedly is doing away with the use of secret passwords. In fact, the hall is being rented for family reunions, concerts for young people, wedding parties, and other purposes with the stipulation that no alcoholic beverages are allowed. An approved kitchen is available. Local scouts and 4-H clubs also use the hall. The New Market Grange is now one of eleven such organizations in Frederick County.

[51] *News-Post,* Frederick, Md., "Grange Offers Range of Activities," July 20, 2003, 19-22.

Masonic Lodge

As mentioned above, the Grange Movement was associated closely with Freemasonry. The Masons were known to have had a Lodge on the William Downey farm on Detrick Road just east of New Market even prior to the American Revolution. Members met there until about 1827 and subsequently in the vicinity of Urbana, also in Frederick County.

Masons in New Market were active in the local Grange. For many years, they also kept a private meeting place in an upstairs room at 19 W. Main Street. Established in 1874, it is known as "Philanthropic Lodge No. 168." Dr. H. Hanford Hopkins was chosen as its first master. The building itself was constructed in 1853 by to the International Order of Odd Fellows for their lodge hall, which they called "Fidelity Lodge No. 54. Later, a group of five local women (Alberta Falconer, Anne Selby, Evelyn Trimble, Dr. Roop's wife, and a fifth lady whose name is not recalled) bought the place and named it "The New Market Social Club." They used the downstairs for a variety of activities and subsequently made the upstairs available as a meeting room for the Masons. Lucien Falconer, Tommy Maher, and Jim Hamilton are among the current members who recall how the building has been used over the years for meetings by various organizations and as a hospitality stop for visitors on town holidays. "The townspeople used to come here to vote on election days," Tommy recalls, "but the Masonic Lodge has always been upstairs." The five ladies eventually sold the building to a holding company controlled by lodge members.

Going up to the meeting room is an adventure not normally accorded to non-members. The stairs are steep and narrow.

Before ascending them, however, one cannot miss a special wall plaque listing ten of this nation's early presidents who were Masons:

George Washington	William Howard Taft
James Buchanan	Andrew Jackson
James Polk	William McKinley
Theodore Roosevelt	Andrew Johnson
James Garfield	Warren Harding

Tommy points out that several subsequent U. S. presidents, including Harry S. Truman, likewise were members of the Masons. Also, Dr. George Riggs, whose accomplishments were described in the previous chapter, was a member of Philanthropic Lodge 168 for fifty years.

The meeting room upstairs, with its dark wood-paneled walls, befits the secrecy, or at least privacy, of the members-only meetings held there for so many years. A number of New Market's highly respected physicians were members of this lodge, including Dr. Jesse W. Downey and his son, Dr. J. W. Downey, as well as Dr. H. H. Hopkins II, who was a lodge master. Among the males in some families, membership in the lodge became a tradition handed down from one generation to another. This was certainly the case in the Zimmerman Family, one of the oldest families still living in New Market. Andrew "Andy" Zimmerman along with his three sons (Paul, Dewey, and Bill) collectively had some 150 years in Masonry. Bill alone was a member of the lodge for seventy years. Paul's grandson Winslow Burhans, the current Mayor of New Market, recalls that this was possible because his Great Uncle Bill lived to be about ninety-three.

The Masonic Lodge in New Market currently lists seventy-two members, and they attend meetings at 7:30 p.m. on the first and third Wednesdays of each month. As the name of this particular lodge implies, it functions as a philanthropic or benevolent organization. Members strive to help each other as needed and to cooperate in charitable enterprises. Current projects include holding fund-raisers to provide scholarships for needy youths as well as supporting the Neo-Natal Unit at the University of Maryland.

Members of Philanthropic Lodge 168 celebrated its 130th anniversary in 2004. Howard Selby claims the distinction of being its "oldest living past master," and his nephew Gregory Selby has held the position since 2003.

CHAPTER 13

"Antiques Capital of Maryland"®

Not until 4 July 1936 did the Town of New Market see its first successful antique shop. A shrewd young entrepreneur by the name of Stoll Kemp started his business on Main Street. The building where he lived and had his business still stands at 14 West Main Street.

The Stoll Kemp Story

Stoll Detrick Kemp was born on 14 October 1904 on his family's farm northwest of Frederick, Maryland.[52] He was the son of David Chester Kemp and Sophia Markell Detrick Kemp.[53] Stoll's father was known as an enterprising and successful businessman who owned a carriage manufacturing business on South Market Street in Frederick. Stoll had two sisters, Ann and Harriet.

While attending The Boys High School in Frederick, Stoll developed an interest in history and genealogy. [54] He learned all that he could about his relatives and ancestors. Stoll continued to study at the University of Maryland and the Baltimore Business

---

[52] *News-Post,* Frederick, Md., article by Tom Johnson entitled, "Stoll D. Kemp Gets His Very Own Day," October 15, 1994, A-1, A-4.
[53] T.J.C. Williams and Folger McKinsey, *History of Frederick County, Maryland, 1967 reprint of 1910 ed, Vol. II, 1251.*
[54] *News-Post, Frederick, Md., article entitled* "'Antiques Capital' Pioneer Dead at 97," November 23, 2001, A-1, A-16.

Stoll Kemp. Jim Birchfield Photo, Courtesy of Dora Connolly.

College. He would prove to be at least as enterprising as his father.

At the height of the Great Depression in July 1930, Stoll moved to New Market and bought the old Hammond Tavern on Main Street for $1,200. Six years later, he established an antique shop in his home. Then, in 1937, Stoll married Katherine Elizabeth Wright, who had a background in art education and had been teaching elementary school teachers. Their marriage evidently was a good match, one that endured for fifty-eight years. They had two daughters, Elizabeth and Ann.

Stoll and Katherine specialized in collecting American-made furniture, decorative pieces, and portraits from the 1700s and 1800s and then sold them from their home business. Lucien Falconer remembers working for Kemp, when Lucien was a boy, many times helping Stoll to deliver pieces of furniture to customers. Howard Selby mentions doing the same kind of work for Stoll and remembers him as being a wonderful man. Since the Kemps had no sons, they had to rely on local boys like Lucien to provide the muscle needed.

Kemp antiques ultimately showed up in art museums and other historic places as well as many private collections along the East Coast. Stoll Kemp's success did not go unnoticed by other antique collectors. He broke the ground for others to follow – and they did! In 1957, Stoll helped to launch the annual fall festival, called "New Market Days," which has brought thousands of antique-lovers to the town. (See Chapter 18, "Annual Celebrations.")

Kemp's accomplishments in New Market are all the more remarkable when one considers the fact that he also served his country as a young naval officer flying reconnaissance missions during World War II. Dora Connelly, owner of "Antiques Folly" at the west end of town, describes Stoll Kemp as "a brilliant man." One can hardly argue with that assessment, given the results that he achieved. He operated his antique business successfully for precisely fifty years - from 4 July 1936 to 4 July 1986 - before retiring. And, by the end of the twentieth century, there were some thirty antique shops in New Market.

Upon their retirement, the Kemps moved to Denton, Maryland, where Mrs. Kemp worked as an art teacher. The Town of New Market honored Stoll in 1994 by proclaiming October 14 (his birthday) as "Stoll D. Kemp Day." His wife died in 1995, but Stoll lived on until passing away on 18 November 2001 at the age of ninety-seven.

A Visit by the First Lady

One Saturday afternoon in February 1968, First Lady Mrs. Lyndon B. Johnson, or "Lady Bird" as she was known, made a shopping trip to New Market with her daughter Lynda Bird and son-in-law Captain Chuck Robb. One of their stops was "Shaw's of New Market," where twelve-year-old Pam Shaw was looking after the shop for her parents, Frank and Shirley Shaw, the owners. Shirley recalls that the special visitors

Antique Shoppers and Sightseers Stroll Down Main Street on a Pleasant
Weekend. Photo Courtesy of Shirley Shaw.

"Antiques Folly."

bought a large pair of old calipers of the kind once used in decorating.

The Washington visitors also shopped at the Old Trail Antique Store owned then by Mrs. Vivian Sponseller. Apparently, Mrs. Robb took a special interest in a Sheraton bookcase, which seemed just right for her old book collection. Unfortunately, Mrs. Sponseller had to tell Lynda Bird that she had sold the case earlier that same day.

Among the other antique shops visited by the First Lady and family members that day were those of Stoll Kemp and also Franklin Rappold. With the passing of time, all of those shops are gone but still are remembered, especially by New Market's old-timers, who may recall that February day when the First Lady came to shop.

Antique Setting at Fleshman's.

Today's Antique Shops in New Market

In 2004, there were twenty-four antique (or associated) shops in town. The number changes as new entrepreneurs arrive or, occasionally, depart.   Ever since the days of Stoll Kemp, antiques seem to be the life-blood of New Market. Why do people become antique dealers, and why do they choose to locate in this particular town?   Dora Connolly cites the fact that her mother was an antique dealer from the time that Dora was four years old. Selling antiques, it would seem, gets into a family's blood.   She had her first antique shop in New Market in the early 1980s. The store was located next to Mealey's Restaurant. In 1993, "Dee," as she often is called, and her husband Bob bought the Victorian home at 105 W.

Main Street from Brinton and Mary Sullivan. Constructed in about 1890, the building replaced an older house. It sits on a large lot close to the elementary school. For the Connollys, it became their home as well as their business - an antique shop, of course. They call it "Antiques Folly." Their Victorian-style house also has been called New Market's "Painted Lady."

Dee points out that, for many years, antiques were narrowly defined as having to be at least 100 years old, whereas now this has been broadened to include items that are pre-World War II or earlier. Collectibles, on the other hand, may include pre-1960 items. She estimates that "Only five percent of the general population are sophisticated enough to appreciate antiques and can afford to buy them." The antiquing business can be expensive. Dee mentions that she attends antique shows up and down the east coast, from Connecticut to Virginia. She indicated that it costs quite a

National Pike Inn During House and Garden Tour of May 1993. Photo Courtesy of Shirley Shaw.

large amount of money just to set up a booth, for example, at the Washington, D.C., Armory and other such sites.

Antique dealers seem to be a closely-knit group of specialized business people. Mrs. Connolly, like many of her counterparts, holds memberships in the Antiques Dealers Association of Maryland ("ADAM") and the Maryland Retailers Association, as well as in the New Market Antiques Dealers Association.

Another Case Study

Rick Fleshman came from Middleburg, Maryland, near Keymar in Carroll County. He played minor-league baseball with a New York Yankees farm club, but an injury kept him from the major leagues. Rick tells how the same thing happened to his father, who had played for a farm club of the old Washington Senators. But baseball wasn't Rick's only interest in those days. He helped his parents "doing antique shows." As he grew up, he wanted to follow in their footsteps, but he decided it would be good to have a business in town so that he would have an income when not doing antique shows. Rick has been in the antique business for over twenty-one years. He has operated his shop in New Market, "Fleshman's Antiques," since January 1989. Located at 2 W. Main Street, it was previously owned by Mildred and Paul Staley, who "had raised six or seven kids in the house," according to Rick. He recalls, "It was the John Kelly General Store before the Staleys owned it."

Why did Rick choose New Market? He says, "I really enjoy it because it is centrally located, I can live in an historic town, put antique pieces in an historic home, and sell them from that location. It's my residence as well as my business." He also appreciates the large barn out in back, for the added storage and workspace it provides. What is it that attracts others to New Market? Rick cites "its consistency, historic charm, Mealey's Restaurant, its linear street layout, really neat architecture, and – it doesn't change very much."

Antique/Other Shops Currently Operating in New Market

Antiques Folly
105 W. Main St.

Glass, China, Ephemera, Black American, Small Furniture

Arlene's Antiques
41 W. Main St.

Quality Antiques

Before Our Time
1 W. Main St.

Formal & Country Furniture, Porcelain, Glass, Silver, Military

The Browsery
55 W. Main St.

Handcrafted Furniture and Accessories

The Chairlift Antiques
84 W. Main St.

Chairs, Chair Sets, Furniture

1812 House
48 W. Main St.

Furniture & Porcelain

Fiacre
22 W. Main St.

Antiques, Reproductions, Classical & Whimsical Home & Garden

Finch's Antiques
122 W. Main St.

Clocks, Furniture, Paintings, Porcelain Sculpture

Fleshman's Antiques
2 W. Main St.

Antique American Oak & Walnut Furniture

Hunting Doll
4 W. Main St.

Unique Jewelry, Designer
Handbags, Hats & Scarves

John L. Due
13 W. Main St.

Antiques, English Country, French
Furniture, Accessories, Clocks

The Little Pottery Shop
75B W. Main St.

Gallery of Hand-Made Pottery

Main Street Antiques
47 W. Main St.

Country Store & Advertising

**Mr. Bob & Andrea's
Antiques**
52 W. Main St.

Mahogany & Oak Furniture,
Porcelain, Glass, Silver & Jewelry

New Market General Store
26 W. Main St.

Country Furniture & Collectibles

The Plug Inn
5 W. Main St.

Lamps, Crystal Fixtures, Home
Lighting & Accessories

Robert Esterly Antiques
20 W. Main St.

Antiques & Restorations

R.P. Brady
3 E. Main St.

Fine Furniture, Paintings

Smith Tavern Antiques
17 E. Main St.

Jewelry, Primitive & Country
Furnishings, Victorian Accessories

Thirsty Knight Antiques
7-9 E. Main St.

Antique Beer Steins, Quality
American Furniture, Collectibles

Thrill of the Hunt Antiques
59 W. Main St.

Antique Furniture & Upholstery

Tomorrow's Antiques   Furniture, Glass, Pottery, Prints &
50 W. Main St.   Collectibles

Victorian Manor   Antique & Estate Jewelry,
33 W. Main St.   Vintage Posters

Yesterday's Treasures   Furniture, Collectibles, Glass,
60 W. Main St.   Silver, Art

Shopping for Antiques

Visitors planning to shop for antiques in New Market would be wise to plan ahead. As a general rule, the antique shops are open on weekends and, during the week, by appointment or "by chance," as one dealer put it. Street guides are available in shops throughout the town, with more detailed information about the hours and specialties of each antique shop as well as places to eat or to stay overnight.

E. Rossig Prints & Custom Framing

Also listed on the New Market street guide, Rossigs is of special interest because of its related services and charming setting. A short walk down Strawberry Alley from the B&B of the same name leads to this very attractive log building from out of the past. It is home to E. Rossig Prints & Custom Framing Shop. The log structure was first built as a house, most likely in the early 1800s, but at a different site nearby on E. Main St.

In the early 1970s, Edgar W. Rossig, Jr., often looked at the log house and thought it might make a nice shop for his framing business, which he had begun in the basement of his Strawberry Inn. He received permission from the town to move the historic building, log by log, to its new location and also to use it as a framing shop. Although this was considered a non-conforming business, the Board of Appeals approved it because the antique dealers in town needed a convenient place where antique pictures could be mounted and framed.

Rossig bought two lots from the former mayor Franklin Smith in 1973 and started moving the logs and putting them together at the new location with his son Bud's help. Bud recalls, "It was a big job. Dad did all the electrical work, plumbing, doors, and trim." Once the basement and fireplace were completed, Rossig began using it for his framing business. Unfortunately, the basement began to fill up with water after a heavy rain, and they had to cover it with a cap in 1978 as a temporary measure until the rest of the log building could be erected. It was finished in 1983.

When Edgar died in 1997, his son "Bud" took over the framing business. Custom framing work still is done on the premises. Bud greets customers in the first-floor studio, where elegant samples of his work are displayed and where visitors, on a cold day, may enjoy the warmth of a brisk fire in its quaint fireplace. The "first floor" actually is up a short flight of stairs leading to the front door.

In the past, Bud also has used the studio for meetings of the New Market Historical Society, over which he presides, and for greeting visitors to the town during annual celebrations.

Rossig's Studio.

Situated between the Strawberry Inn B&B and Rossig's studio, the Rossig gazebo is often a gathering place for New Market festivities.

CHAPTER 14

Local Government

On 28 March 1878, eighty-five years after Nicholas Hall started selling lots in New Market, the Town was incorporated by an act of the Maryland State Legislature. After Governor John L. Carroll signed the legislation and an election was held, Isaac Russell took office as the first mayor of New Market, but he served in office for only two years.

At the same time, a town council was established, and it was made up of three commissioners: Harry W. Dorsey, Dr. H. Hanford Hopkins, and J. T. P. Mount. The council continues to the present day, with five members now being elected every four years. Traditionally, the council has concerned itself with such issues as street and sidewalk maintenance, zoning and covenant matters, local taxes, water and sewage issues, annexation proposals, and efforts to maintain the architecture and traditions of this small town. Town meetings are held on the second Wednesday of each month in the Town Hall at 39 W. Main Street, and they are open to the public. Mayoral elections likewise are held every four years. The mayor may attend town council meetings and take part in deliberations. He does not have a vote, but he has veto power over certain ordinances adopted by the council. Council members, however, may override such a veto with at least a four-fifths vote.

In the 127 years since Mayor Russell took office, twenty
mayors have served, with an average term of just over six
years. Most remarkable, however, is the fact that two New
Market mayors served for almost forty-nine of those years.
They were Wm. Franklin Smith, who was mayor from 1949
to1969 and Franklin Shaw, New Market mayor from 1969 to
1998. Perhaps it should be called the "Franklin Period" in
the history of New Market.

I had to reach up high to sound the front door knocker on Franklin
Smith's home in New Market. It was the afternoon of 25 November
2002, and I heard a husky voice say, "Come on in!" I did so and found
Smith just inside. "I am the oldest" (in town), he announced, obviously
proud to be eighty-eight at the time. His wife, Grace, had been dead
for thirteen years. They had one son, Wayne, and two grandsons – one
in Russia in the computer business and one in Boston in banking.
Wayne is a planner in the Frederick area but previously was an
architect and designed Frank's house, which I was visiting. Frank said
he liked its openness, and I did too.

Frank mentioned that he grew up
on a farm in the New Market area.
In 1942, Smith bought the house
that is now the Strawberry Inn Bed
and Breakfast at 17 West Main
Street. He paid $1,800 for it, lived
there for thirty-four years and then
sold it to Edgar and Jane Rossig.
He was in the cattle business in the
1960s and 1970s. He had one farm
to the east of town, another on
Ijamsville Road, and a third on
Boyer's Mill Road.   In earlier
years, Frank kept horses for pulling
wagons. At the time I visited
Frank, he still had about seventy-
five cattle.   - JFS

Mayor Franklin Smith

New Market Town Hall.

Mayor Franklin Smith

As previously mentioned, Franklin Smith was the mayor of New Market from 1949 to 1969, but he has been active in town politics continuously for much longer than that. In fact, he was honored at a special surprise dinner at Mealey's Restaurant on 13 September 1999 "for his over forty-six years of government service." Smith still serves on the Planning and Zoning Commission by appointment. As chief among his accomplishments as Mayor, Franklin cited the fact that he had helped to organize a fire company and build a firehouse in the late 1950s. He described how they developed a fire pond of reserve water by digging a large hole and shoring up the banks with logs. This effort would lead to the development of the larger fire pond north of town that still is in use today.

The ex-mayor recalled when all the antique shops came to town. "We once had around forty shops," he said. As for the future, Smith observed, "You got to make up your mind whether New Market continues as 'Antiques Capital of Maryland'® or you let other businesses in." Asked whether the town "can't have its cake and eat it too?" he replied, "That's for sure!" As for town zoning and covenants, Franklin said they are "good - if enforced for everybody."

Mayor Franklin Shaw

Franklin Smith would have been a hard act to follow for most local politicians, but the New Market voters found their man - and then some - in Mayor Franklin Shaw.[55] He took office on 14 May 1969 and served as mayor until his death in 1998. Throughout all those years, he dedicated himself to serving his community and refused steadfastly to accept a salary. His almost thirty-year stint as mayor is unmatched

But his remarkable career began much earlier, far away from New Market, Maryland. In the early 1950s, Frank served in the U.S. Army during the Korean War. He was wounded while there and received the Purple Heart. Frank became a medic in the first Mobile Army Surgical Hospital (MASH) unit while in Korea. In fact, his service there preceded that of the colonel who wrote the story for the movie "MASH."

Mayor Shaw. Photo Courtesy of Shirley Shaw.

[55] Bruce Hamilton, *News-Post,* Frederick, Md., "Mayor Shaw, 68, Dies," May 21, 1998.

Frank's military service continued in Japan, where he was assigned to work at Osaka General Hospital. While there, he somehow found time to help organize a local orphanage. He also managed to take courses at Tokyo University and became rather fluent in Japanese. After returning to the United States, Frank was assigned to Fort Lee, Virginia, where he learned to fly and qualified as a pilot. Years later he kept a plane at Frederick Airport and continued the sport of flying when he could find the time.

After leaving the Army, Frank returned to his home state and went on with his education, attending Western Maryland College and the University of Maryland.

Dancing was one of Frank's favorite pursuits, and so it was during this period of his life that he became an instructor with the Arthur Murray Studio in Washington, making appearances on national television more than once.

It was at the University of Maryland that Shaw met his sweetheart, Shirley Bussard. Their 1954 wedding took place in Ellicott City, and their first daughter, Pamela, was born in 1955. Frank later used his battlefield experience as a medic to become a lab technician at Frederick Memorial Hospital. He delivered their second baby, Lori, there in 1959. Shirley had been in training to become a nurse, but in those days one could not marry while in nursing school. So she gave up nursing to marry Frank and went to work for the telephone company. Meanwhile, Frank earned a graduate degree in biochemistry from Shepherd College and worked at a medical lab in Hagerstown on Fridays and Saturdays. Subsequently, he helped to establish the first outpatient medical lab in Frederick on Toll House Road. It was known as the Community Medical Lab. Later, Quest Diagnostics, Inc. purchased the lab and still operates at that location.

Following this experience, Frank took a job in 1961 at Fort
Detrick in Frederick. Assigned to the Army's medical unit
there, he worked in the Pathology-Biophysics Division.
Two years later he received recognition in the Journal of
Experimental Medicine for his work with the anthrax virus,
then known as an infectious disease of cattle and sheep and
now for its recent notoriety as a biological warfare threat.

It was during his time living in Frederick that Frank became
interested in antiques. He and his wife would venture into
New Market often to look and sometimes buy. Gradually
they accumulated things of interest and of value.

Shirley Shaw recalls her own early interest in antiques: "As
a little girl, I used to come here to New Market. Mother had
antiques." Later, she and Frank lived in an apartment on
South Street with antiques in the hallway and all the way up
the steps and in the apartment. She tells how she and Frank
happened to move to New Market:

> *There was a Dr. Ralph Michaels who lived there.*
> *Frank knew him from working at Frederick*
> *Memorial Hospital. The doctor used to say, "Those*
> *people in New Market are crazy. I will sell my house*
> *to you." But we did not have the money. So he*
> *asked us, "Would you move into that house and run*
> *an antique shop for me?"*

The house to which he referred was at 2 W. Main Street and
was owned by Paul Staley at the time. The Shaws rented it
and sold antiques there until later convincing Dr. Michaels
to sell his house to them "for a price," according to Shirley.
It became their dream house – an antique shop that became
known as "Shaws of New Market." Shirley recalls that

Frank placed an advertisement at his school to help them sell their antiques. As time went on, Frank earned a fine reputation for his knowledge of antiques and their restoration. He was a member of the New Market Antique Dealers Association for many years.

Frank Shaw served as a town council member in New Market for four years before becoming mayor. Shirley says that the town had become run-down, and Frank was determined to improve things. She recalls:

> *Frank got along with almost everybody. He loved that mayor's job. He often would come home, have dinner, and then go back to his office until ten or eleven o'clock at night. I would sometimes walk down to see if he was okay.*

As for his legacy as mayor, Shirley points to the establishment of the Historic District Commission and the Planning and Zoning Commission "and seeing that people comply." It is no accident that New Market maintained its historic character and presence in a changing world during Shaw's long tenure as mayor. He also belonged to the Council of Governments and served for a time as its president. As a member of the Maryland Municipal League, he was inducted into the Public Service Hall of Fame in 1997. Frank Shaw was mayor of New Market also during the town's bicentennial celebration in 1993.

Like the David of biblical fame, Shaw was not reluctant to take on a giant. He struggled successfully to prevent a truck stop facility from being established at the Route 75 eastern entrance to New Market, and he held off McDonalds

Restaurant chain when they attempted to install its signature arches in the same location.

Frank died, following a heart attack, on 19 May 1998 at the age of sixty-eight.[56]

Mayor Rick Fleshman

Following the death of Franklin Shaw, the town council appointed Richard "Rick" Fleshman to serve out the remaining three years of Shaw's term as mayor. Fleshman previously had chaired the Planning and Zoning Commission there. Asked what his biggest accomplishment as mayor was, Rick said, "Nothing changed here. The preservation of the town continued." But he added that there was one big policy change in that he started the town in the direction of getting the county to supply New Market with water rather than the town trying to get its own water treatment.

Protecting New Market's historic nature was important to Mayor Fleshman, but he is remembered also for his particular initiative with respect to recreation facilities in the town's community park. He was successful in obtaining a state grant to obtain swing sets and other playground equipment. This involved much research and work on his part, for example, with respect to safety engineering and specifications for the equipment.

Mayor Winslow Burhans

Winslow "Wynn" Burhans III defeated Fleshman for mayor in the next election and is currently serving that four-year term. Town Council members include Terri Houston, Rita

---

[56] *Gazette,* New Market, Md., obituary, May 28, 1998.

Mueller, Kathleen Snowden, Robert Parker, and Haley Tate. The next New Market election is scheduled for May 2005.

The Burhans Administration has reported accomplishments in the areas of traffic control, street safety, and planning for the future of the town. Specifically, in Mayor Burhans' November 2002 newsletter, he cited the approval for execution of a Water Service Area Agreement, adding that "This is a long awaited resolution for town water." This agreement, which was executed on 29 April 2003, allows for the "incremental construction of a county-owned water distribution system" within the Town of New Market to provide a water supply for the community's immediate and long-term needs. It promises to provide the town with a defined water system capacity for both the existing population and planned growth within the Town of New Market. The agreement addresses such an allocation for the existing and planned development within the current town boundaries, including the Brinkley Manor and Royal Oaks developments, but future developments or annexations will require an amendment to this agreement.

Annexation Approved

On 14 April 2004, the Town Council reached an agreement for the annexation of some 58 acres of land just east of the existing town limits along Route 144. The annexation is to include forty-nine acres of the Orchard at New Market LLC, just west of Route 75, per an agreement with the developer, Steve Seawright of the Seawright Corporation of Bethesda, Maryland. Plans call for 104 homes to be built over several years along with the hilltop there being reserved for sports use. An additional parcel of land on the east side of the road is being reserved for commercial use.

June Snowden's Stone House.

CHAPTER 15

The Schools of New Market

Early Schools

In the nineteenth century, public schools in New Market, as elsewhere in the nation, were segregated. One of the first schools in town was a one-room log schoolhouse at the east end of town. African-American children received their primary education in New Market at this school. Chestnut logs were used for the walls and the plastered ceilings, and the floorboards likewise were made of chestnut. The place was built as a home about 200 years ago but began to be used as a school in about 1850. Reportedly, this school had only four students during its final year.

Luther Peach bought the property in 1887, selling it a few years later to William O. Lee, who gave it to his daughter Florence Lee and son-in-law Reginald Snowden in 1920 as a wedding present. The couple raised eight children in this small home. To make it more habitable, Mr. Snowden continually made improvements. For example, he added two bedrooms and a summer-kitchen stone hearth dividing the two rooms downstairs, and a small kitchen in the back.

Later, after Reginald's wife passed away, his widowed daughter, June Snowden, came to live with him along with her five children. After her father died, June became co-owner of the home along with her twin brother, Julius

Snowden. She continued to make improvements in the house as her father had done. For example, with the help of a local carpenter, she covered the outside of the house with stones gathered from old building sites in town. June remembers how she and her five children helped by carrying the stones home. Later, she added a stone hearth between the two bedrooms. Altogether, they produced a very unique building in New Market and a charming little home.

June Snowden takes much pride in the fact that she still lives in the simple log home where she was born and where she raised her own children. She has left the original chestnut log walls exposed in her small living room because she treasures them for their age and the memories of many years. Likewise, June cherishes many family heirlooms, including two antique pictures that had belonged to her mother. Despite the fact that the ceilings are low, the rooms are small, and there is never enough room to store things, she loves her home and wants to spend the rest of her life there. June marvels that her parents were able to raise their eight children in this small home, but she notes that they were all born about four years apart from each other. By the time the youngest of them arrived, the older ones were old enough to move out. "There were never more than four children living here at one time," she explains.

This historic former schoolhouse and home, located at 15 East Main St., is one of the first attractions seen by visitors who approach New Market from the east.

Nearly right around the corner, at 1 N. Federal Street, stands another former schoolhouse. It was constructed of stone in about 1868. For many years, it was the primary school for white youngsters in New Market until a more permanent elementary school was built at the opposite end of town. Dr. H. Hanford Hopkins IV describes the "no nonsense" discipline at the New Market School, which he attended in the very early 1900s. On the other hand, he described the spelling bees conducted there as "the most fun in the school." The youngsters played ball in the schoolyard and even built a clay court for tennis, according to Hopkins.

Subsequently, this stone building was turned over to the education of black children in town. The current stone-and-frame building replaced the former all-stone structure in the 1940s, when it became a two-room school for black children.

June Snowden remembers the school on Federal Street. It was her grade school. She even remembers her first teacher there, Miss Alice Delauder, who taught first- through third-grade students. Florence (Thomas) Awkaid taught grades four through six, June recalls. Another teacher at the black school was Janie Davis. The room on the left was for the first three grades, and the room on the right, where there are two windows, was for the upper grades. A playground and outhouses were out back of the school. Two coal stoves heated the school, and the coal was stored just inside the cellar door on the right side of the building.

After completing grade school here, its black students usually went on to attend Lincoln High School in Frederick (now known as West Frederick), according to Ms. Snowden.

When Frederick County schools were desegregated in 1961-62, this school was closed, and its students enrolled in New Market Elementary.

Schools of Today

Within the town limits, there currently are two public schools: New Market Elementary and New Market Middle School. They are located next to each other off of Main Street and across from the firehouse at the west end of town. Additionally, there are three nearby schools serving the general vicinity of New Market. These include Deer Crossing Elementary (1 ½ miles northwest of town on Boyer's Mill Road) as well as Oakdale Elementary and Middle Schools, which are collocated 2 ½ miles west of New Market on the Old National Pike (Route 144). Most high school students living in the vicinity of New Market attend Linganore High School on Old Annapolis Road off of Route 75 and about four miles north of New Market.

New Market Elementary School

Not many people know as much about the history of the New Market Elementary School as Betty Jeffers (Mrs. Mark Jeffers) of nearby Monrovia. Betty not only was one of the school's early graduates, but she also had her daughters educated there, worked at the school herself for 31 years, and now has a daughter teaching there.

She was Betty Davis in those days. She began her education at New Market Elementary in 1936. It was the original school, which was built in 1932. Betty recalls that there were eight rooms altogether – seven classrooms and an eighth room used as a cafeteria. A small auditorium was just to the left of the entrance to the school. Unlike the situation in schools today, each classroom had a cloakroom in the rear. The school also featured a large nearby playground as well as a baseball diamond that was used by local adults as

New Market Elementary School Graduating Class of 1944. Photo Courtesy of Betty Jeffers.

well as school children. Nearby there was a cornfield. William Brown was the principal back then. Betty says, "He was called 'Pappy' by the kids."

She also remembers that the school drew students from in and around New Market and from as far away as Route 80 to the south and the Penn Shop Road area, to the east near Mt. Airy. The school had only seven grades then. She and other graduates of the school would go on to Frederick High School for grades eight through eleven. Shortly after this period, seventh-grade graduates went on to the Elm Street School (the old Frederick High) for one year only before entering the newly built Frederick High School, according to one such student, Paul Zimmerman, Jr.

Betty cherishes the photograph she still has of her seventh-grade graduating class of 1943-44. (See photo on previous page.) All thirty-one students can be seen standing, perhaps in their best clothes, on the front steps of the small brick schoolhouse.

In subsequent years, of course, more classrooms were needed, and an addition opened in 1962. "Our daughter Leslie started school there at that time," Betty well recalls. And so her own association with the school was resumed as both daughters, Leslie and Teresa, worked their way through the grades. Then, in 1966, Betty accepted a position as secretary at the school. "The principal talked me into it," she says, "but it was the best job I ever had."

Betty recalls that Mary Wood, the descendant of New Market founder Nicholas Hall mentioned in Chapter 2, was a teacher at New Market Elementary School.

The school went through two additional phases of expansion in 1976 and 1978. Current enrollment for the 2003-2004 school year was listed as 468. The principal is Linda Hezlep.

Betty Jeffers stayed at New Market Elementary until retiring in 1997. She is proud to have her daughter Teresa teaching there currently, and she noted, "Teresa teaches fourth grade in the same classroom that I had when I was in fourth grade."

New Market Middle School

The New Market Middle School was established in 1979, according to George Helta, who has been teaching there from its founding days. Built to accommodate 900 students, it was one of the largest middle schools in Frederick County at that time. George notes that the school's first principal was Tom Shade. Prior to that, from about 1964 to 1979, local students in grades 7 through 12 were taught at Linganore High School. George believes that all the Frederick County High Schools included those grades back then.

The New Market Middle School accommodates students from the east side of Boyer's Mill Road through New Market and all the way to the Frederick County part of Mt. Airy, as well as the area north including Libertytown, Unionville, and Johnsville. The school's population has fluctuated with changes in its boundaries. Prior to the opening of the Oakdale Middle School in 2000, for example, the New Market Middle School became so overcrowded that it became necessary to add thirteen portable classrooms on campus. George recalls that these portables were in use for seventh graders over about five years and came to be known as "The Thirteen Colonies." Two of the portable classrooms are still in use as sixth-grade classrooms. Currently, Carolyn

Kimberlin is the Principal of New Market Middle School. Its graduates routinely enroll at Linganore High School. For this reason, the student body in New Market has chosen the same black and red school colors as at Linganore High, replacing the blue and gray of former years.

CHAPTER 16

New Market Post Office

The local post office dates to the year 1800. John Hall, the brother of New Market founder Nicholas Hall, served as its first postmaster. For most of the years since then, the post office was located either in the home of the postmaster or in some other building along Main Street. Its last location there was at the Town Hall at 39 W. Main St. up until the time that a new and modern facility was built and put into service at the west end of town (i.e., 168 W. Main St.). The new post office began serving New Market on 6 January 1993. The current postmaster is Patricia Barger. She says that the number of deliveries currently is drastically different from years past. She stated, "In New Market (i.e., Zip Code 21774), we now deliver to 3,428 individual houses plus 509 post office boxes."

In 1992, former Postmaster Ida Lu (Price) Brown, who held that office from 1979 to 1981, wrote a very comprehensive and colorful history of the New Market Post Office. She described the development of postal services from colonial times and listed some thirty-three postmasters who served New Market from 1800 through 1981. One of these, Ida's immediate predecessor, was Hilda Brashear Free (now deceased), who served more than seventeen years as postmaster. Her husband, Monroe Free, moved to Frederick but maintained a close relationship with many friends in New Market until he too passed away in 2004.

Ida Lu Brown's fine work is on file with the New Market Historical
Society.   When interviewed at her current home in Frederick,
Maryland, on 30 April 2004, Ida Lu very graciously agreed to the use
of information from her post office history in this book.   - JFS

Mrs. Brown points out that, when Nicholas Hall and William
Plummer were beginning to offer lots for sale in New
Market, there already were seventy-five U.S. post offices,
including ten in Maryland. The U.S. Post Office Department
was established in 1789.

Unidentified Early New Market Postmaster at Work. Photo Courtesy of Dora
Connolly.

New Market Postmasters
(As Compiled by Ida Lu (Price) Brown)

1800	John Hall	1907	John T.P. Mount
1803	Richard Roberts	1909	Andrew J. Zimmerman
1815	Jacob Houch	1914	Bayard C. Burgess
1817	John H.M. Smith	1937	Leroy J. Hoff (temp.)
1818	Jacob Houch		Blanch Howard
1822	Joseph Summers		(Commissioned, but never
1823	Thomas Anderson		served)
1841	Hamilton Stier		Mrs. Olive Sponseller
1845	William P. Anderson	1943	Edith Kindley (until
1849	Hamilton Stier		September) Hilda
1853	Absolom Anderson		Brashear (Commissioned
1856	William Downey, Jr.		in 1944)
1861	Hamilton Stier	1946	Frances Brashear
1865	Oliver P. Snyder (3 mos.)	1961	Hilda Brashear Free
1865	Hamilton Stier	1978	A. Retta Peiffer
1870	Pliney O.H. Stier		Tammy Davis
1880	Ida P. Stier		John C. Munson
1901	New Market, a station of		(all officers-in-charge)
	Monrovia, served by rural	1979	Ida L. Price (Brown)
	carrier	1981	Lavinia McGolerick

Local Post Office Established

It was on 7 February 1800 that John Hall took office as New Market's first postmaster. His was a political appointment as was the case then and for many years thereafter, according to Ida Lu's historical account. Hall's political preferences with the Federalist Party coincided with those of our second U.S. President, John Adams, in office then. It was the year that the Post Office Department was moved to Washington, D.C., and also was during a period when many post offices were being established.

In her historical account, Ida Lu states that the first New Market Post Office is believed to have been located in

Postmark Used During Annual Celebrations. Courtesy of Ida Lu Brown.

Postmaster Hall's home at 41 W. Main St., which is now and has been for some years an antique shop. Known as "Arlene's Antiques," it is owned by Mrs. Arlene Gue.

Two years after Thomas Jefferson became president, Richard Roberts was appointed to replace Hall as postmaster in New Market. The year was 1803, the same year as the Louisiana Purchase. The additional territories doubled the size of our young nation. The National Road was being built, making travel easier, and linking eastern communities with the new frontier to the west. It was only a year later that explorers Lewis and Clark would set out on their northwest expedition. Roberts continued his tenure as postmaster through the War of 1812.

Express Mail Comes to Town

Mail carriers in those early times would arrive on horseback, horse and rider both exhausted after a long and arduous ride. Horns would be blown to alert the postmaster and residents of their arrival. While the rider changed to a fresh mount, the postmaster would exchange the outgoing for incoming mail. Then, back in the saddle, the carrier would ride on to his next point of delivery.

Early Salaries and Postal Rates

Postmaster John H.M. Smith received $82.12 as compensation in 1817, presumably for the year. By 1823, when twenty-one-year-old Thomas Anderson was postmaster, the annual salary had risen to $102.83. More than a century later, Postmaster Olive Sponseller received a salary of $693. It is quite apparent that dedicated public servants filled these positions, instead of seeking a quick path to wealth.

First-class postage cost two cents in 1885, eventually climbed to three cents, and, rather remarkably stayed at that rate through half of the twentieth century.

Postmaster – Not "Postmistress"

Mrs. Brown covets her former official title as Postmaster and disdains someone calling a woman who holds this position a "Postmistress" - as, she recalls, some people did in years past. She should know, after thirty years with the Postal Service. Ida Lu was Postmaster in Barnesville, Maryland, for twenty-eight years before moving to Frederick. Then, in

1979, she accepted the position of Postmaster in New Market and commuted there every day from Frederick.

Ida Lu recalls that the New Market Post Office years ago was located at the former National Pike Inn at 9-11 W. Main St. Later, it again became the practice to have the post office in the home of the postmaster. For example, Hilda and Monroe Free maintained the facility in their home at 45-47 W. Main Street from 1961 to 1978. The facility remained in the Free house for some years even after they had moved. In 1984, however, the homeowner, Mary Harrington, did not renew the lease, and the post office was moved to the Town Hall where it remained until 1993.

Such postmasters as Mrs. Free and Mrs. Brown were exceptional women, carrying out their official duties on a daily basis while caring for their families as well. Ida Lu, for example, raised ten children during her long career with the Postal Service. "Many times I would be putting mail into the slots with one hand and rocking the cradle with the other," she recalls. In her case, keeping the post office in her home was the only way. In this excerpt from her historical account, Ida Lu touches on some of her experiences as "Postmaster-Mom: "

> *All sorts of merchandise came through the mails that caused excitement. It was no problem getting the kids up for school when the baby chicks arrived (i.e., in the mail). They would hear the chirping and come rushing down to poke little fingers in the holes so the hungry chicks would peck at them. Once I think I nearly killed a baby alligator the truck driver handed me very tenderly as he announced softly the contents of the miniature crate. Many is the time a baby doll*

(nude) would fall out of the way pouch that each office opened to remove mail for that office from the main dispatch office in Rockville. It was being returned to its mommy in Barnesville, after being dropped in the sack days before by a teasing brother!

Ida Lu explains that local residents have post office boxes assigned to them at the post office, where they have to pick up their mail. Strictly speaking, mail addressed to their street addresses without a box number is to be returned, but as she discovered when she took on the job in 1979, "You don't go by the book in New Market." Some individuals would become very upset if they made the trip to pick up their mail only to find that it had been returned to the sender for lack of a box number. The number of households in town is small enough so that it makes sense just to drop the mail in the assigned box.

"I certainly enjoyed being Postmaster in New Market," Ida Lu exclaims, adding: "It was wonderful; the people were so nice."

Village Tea Room.

CHAPTER 17

Village Tea Room

The Village Tea Room Restaurant is at 81 W. Main Street. That places it on the north side of the street and at the far west end of town - the part of New Market that was owned by William Plummer in 1790. The restaurant sits on lots 12 and 13, which Plummer sold to his son Isaac and Isaac's partner, Anthony Poultney. As mentioned previously, Poultney owned a sawmill in nearby Monrovia. Poultney and his wife Mary were known to be prosperous residents of New Market, where they also ran a button factory.

John Pearce purchased the property in 1848. It had only a log house on it then. When he died only fourteen years later, the land and the log house were inherited by Maria Pearce, his widow, and their three daughters: Eliza, Cinderella (called "Cinnie") and Lydia. Later, Eliza married Henry Rhodes, a well-known flour dealer. It was Rhodes who built the current Victorian structure. After he died in 1892, Maria Pearce began making use of the house as a girls' finishing school. Maria lived until age ninety, and so did her daughter Cinnie, who taught school in New Market for a long time.

The property remained with the Pearce Family until 1934, when Luther and Annie Stull bought it. Their son Emory and his wife Daisy became the owners in 1943 and began selling antiques there, just seven years after Stoll Kemp opened the first antique shop in New Market. Later, James and Marie Hutsel bought the property. In 1975, they opened a bakery and called it "The Country Kitchen." The following year they added a tearoom, still under the same name.

Paul L. Davis took over the establishment in 1984, built an addition to the original building in 1989, and renamed the business "The Village Tea Room." The current ownership team of Craig A. and Carla J. Wolf bought it from Davis in September 1998 and expanded the tearoom into a full-service restaurant specializing in country cooking. It is open Tuesday through Thursday from 11 a.m. to 3 p.m., on Fridays and Saturdays from 11 a.m. to 8 p.m., and on Sundays from 11 a.m. to 5 p.m. As the couple notes in their menu: "We can accommodate groups from two to fifty."

Customers can dine inside in a smoke-free environment or, in suitable weather, outdoors with a garden view. The menu features local names such as "The Linganore" (grilled chicken breast topped with ham and melted Swiss cheese on a toasted roll) or "The Monocacy" (hearty stew served in a bread bowl). Then there is the aroma coming from the kitchen of freshly baked pies, muffins, and other baked goods. The Plummers and Poultneys could not have foreseen what they started with this property on West Main Street.

The Wolfs have two children, Jennifer and Josh. At times, they seem to have heard mysterious noises in the old house, for example, the sound of a key turning or a door closing. Carla tells how she has had some fun with the youngsters over this in years past, telling them that it must be the ghost of Lydia Pearce. Other New Market residents have told of similar experiences in their 200-year-old homes.

CHAPTER 18

Annual Celebrations

Small towns across our nation find ways to take time off at least once a year to celebrate their existence, have fun, welcome visitors, and perhaps display their wares for sale. Music, food, merriment, and activities abound. For New Market, Maryland, the attractions are its many antique shops and the more than 200-year-old town itself. It is a place where visitors can come and bring their children to see what it was like to live many years ago.

Franklin Smith was the mayor in 1957 when the town decided to establish "A Day in New Market," as it was called then. It happened to be a Tuesday, 28 May. It was a beginning.

New Market Days

By 1960, the town's leaders were starting to think big. This time they staged their event on a Wednesday, 12 October, and called it "New Market Day." Although they had not yet chosen to go to a weekend celebration, it was Columbus Day, a national holiday.

Nick Wood recalls that his father, Charles Wood, was one of those that started the event. According to Nick, the group also included Stoll Kemp, Dorsey Griffith, B.E. Sullivan,

Frank Shaw, and Commander Messanelle, after whom Messanelle Memorial Park in New Market is named.

New Market had sixteen antique shops by then. Visitors could browse and buy all day long if they wished. New Market Day, however, offered much more than that. There were demonstrations of apple butter cooking, quilting, basket and wicker weaving, harness making, and displays of firearms and edged weapons. Visitors also learned the traditional way of baking Maryland beaten biscuits, using country-kitchen implements and methods. For example, the biscuit dough actually is beaten with a hammer, or even the back of an axe (see photo in chapter 18.) Adding color and

Troubador John Durant Entertains During New Market Days Celebration.

1961 Poster. Courtesy of Shirley Shaw.

excitement to the event were the horse and buggy rides. Riding down Main Street in a surrey with the fringe on top while listening to the "clippity-clop" of the horse's hoofs made for a perfect day.

The following day, it was reported in **The Baltimore Sun** that the event drew "several thousand visitors" to New Market. Individual antique shop proprietors estimated that up to 1,000 visitors came to their shops, and the Volunteer Fire Department reported serving 1,200 dinners.

Program for "A Day in New Market," May 28, 1957

10 a.m. Grange Hall   Welcome to New Market by Mayor W. Franklin
Smith.

10:45   Late Eighteenth Century Flower Arrangements
Art of drying material for Winter Bouquets
Mrs. Asa Watkins and Mrs. Frank Harris

10:45   Town Hall
Antiques, privately owned on exhibit.
Short discussions on Industries and Imports of the period.
Mr. Charles Wood, descendant of earliest settlers of New Market
and Mr. Marshall Etchison, authority on antiques.
Both of these gentlemen are past presidents of the Frederick
County Historical Society.
Visit Grace Episcopal Church, Rev. John Rollman, rector.

11:30 to 2:30   Luncheon will be served at Mealey's Hotel.
Effort will be made to avoid loss of time if you cannot
be served immediately.

2:30   Grange Hall – Talk on Antiques.

2:30   Town Hall – Flower Arrangements.
These talks will be repeated in order that all may be
accommodated. Displays will be in both halls and open all day.

The following Shops, all in interesting houses, will welcome
you. Appropriate Flower Arrangements are in each.

1. Mr. and Mrs. Stoll D. Kemp. The Kemp family were among
the early county settlers. A beautiful home and antiques of
quality.

2. Mr. and Mrs. Frank Perham. Fine antiques, well displayed.
The house, with a large boxwood, has exterior and interior
interest.

3. Surch House. Mr. and Mrs. Morse. Interesting small items
displayed in an old house.

4. Mr. and Mrs. Ray Messanelle specialize in Chinese and Oriental containers.

5. Mr. and Mrs. Dorsey Griffith. Both the Dorsey and the Griffith names appear on the earliest New Market records. Interesting house built in three parts. Fine antiques.

3:30   New Market Methodist Church, Rev. Lowell S. Garland, pastor. Short talk on the restoration of the building by Charles F. Bowers.

Songs by Mrs. Paul Keppel (Florence Kirk). She was for five years leading coloratura with the Metropolitan Opera Company. Mrs. Keppel has been living in Maryland since she returned from residence abroad.

Browningsville Cornet Band on Parade. Photo Courtesy of Shirley Shaw.

With such success, New Market Day became an annual event and was extended to two or three days over a weekend each year, in September or October. Thus it came to be called "New Market Days." After more than forty years, this event truly has become a lasting tradition.

Harmony Cornet Band Performs During New Market Days.

New Market Days are for Kids (Actually Dolls) Too. Photo Courtesy of Shirley Shaw (1997).

All Kinds of Fun With Roping Tricks By "Cowboy" Ron McGinley of Frederick.

"Moon Sisters" Make An Appearance in 2004.

The Art of Quilting.

Marjorie Hammond
Demonstrates Making
"Beaten Biscuits."

Basket Weaving Demonstrated.

Making
Apple Butter.

Bonnets Galore.

Music has been an important ingredient of New Market Days. "The Barnstormers Trio," for example, has performed there for years. The group includes Tom Jolin on the hammered dulcimer, fiddler John Winship, and guitarist Slim Harrison. Then there was a group called "The Orchard Boys," who played Bluegrass tunes. Others entertained with country music, Dixieland, or Scottish bagpipes. John Durant, a strolling colonial troubadour, has been a very popular entertainer at New Market Days for many years – as has storyteller Betty Jackson, known for her "Miss Betty's Colonial Trunk" featuring stories for children in the town's park.

Teaching youngsters, and even adults, about the past is integral to this annual celebration. Visiting the New Market General Store; watching demonstrators make soap, weave wicker baskets and cane chair seats; or visiting the Civil War encampment at the end of Strawberry Alley makes for a very interesting and enjoyable weekend. Then there is the food: the homemade chicken corn soup, barbecued beef and country ham sandwiches offered at the New Market Grange; funnel cakes by the Lions Club; traditional turkey, ham, and oyster dinners at the Fire Hall; homemade ice cream and lemonade; or perhaps dinner at Mealey's Restaurant on Main Street. All of the local churches likewise participate with food stands offering soups, sandwiches, and desserts.

Local Artist Mrs. William Hill.

Old Time Traffic From New Market Days 2004.

Happ Allison Plays His Dulcimer.

On occasion, an uninvited guest might appear at New Market Days. In 1989, it was the aftermath of Hurricane Hugo. Friday 22 September, the first day of the celebration, was a nice warm day. On Saturday, however, a bad storm arrived with chilling winds and rain. Visitors, who were not deterred, were rewarded with blue skies and nice fall weather on Sunday. In any case, New Market Days goes on, rain or shine.

"The 44th Annual New Market Days" celebration was held on 3,4, and 5 October 2003. Rita Mueller of Grange Hall Antiques was in charge of planning this event. Scheduling the event in early October, instead of September as in most previous years, turned out to be fortuitous. Hurricane Isabel wreaked much havoc throughout the entire area in late September. The damage, disruption, flooding, and extended power outages that occurred then well might have caused

New Market Days to be cancelled. As it turned out, however, the first weekend in October was characterized by suitable fall weather. A bit of coolness in the air only helped the sale of warm food, such as the "Slippery Slope Soup" and hot cider.

Featured entertainers at the event recently included the "Moon Sisters," historic re-enactors, who performed in the town hall to the delight of visitors. Period performers such as Civil War "spy" Lottie Moon Clark, her husband Judge James Clark, and Lottie's sister, Ginnie Moon, described their wartime adventures and personal experiences back then. The two sisters claimed to have been engaged to be married a total of forty-eight times, between the two of them. The group never came out of character, and the audience loved it.

As in many years past, there was a parade through town on Saturday. Local fire trucks led the way, with Civil War re-enactors marching behind, followed by other marchers and the Yellow Springs Concert Band. Musicians also performed along Main Street. Visitors brought their children to witness what life was like in the old days and perhaps have a pony ride. The adults roamed the many antique shops filled with old treasures. The parking lots all were at their fullest on Sunday, especially the one behind Mealey's Restaurant, where diners could choose between a special brunch or a full-course dinner. Others chose to eat along the way, for instance, at the Village Tea Room, the Grange, or the General Store. Business was very good. Once more, New Market Days proved to be a very pleasant place for a family outing in rural America.

The "New Market Days Heritage & Crafts Festival" of 2004 similarly took place on the first weekend in October. Its organizer, Rita Mueller, however, promises a return to the tradition of holding this event "during the last weekend in September for good!" Rita adds that this is now "written in stone and not to be changed in the future by committees."

Christmas In New Market

The holiday spirit abounds in early December each year. It is a time when local residents and shopkeepers welcome visitors in a special way. For those who come, it is a unique chance to experience what it would have been like to be in a small town in the nineteenth century during the holidays. Additionally, this historic Maryland town affords a distinct opportunity for holiday shoppers to look for gifts and antiques in a host of conveniently collocated shops.

Christmas Choir Singing Carols in Messanelle Park.

Gary Gregg (Soprano Sax), Rick Bowe (Banjo), and Kevin Olivera (Tuba)
Perform During New Market Days in 2003.

It was Jane Rossig, Innkeeper of the Strawberry Inn Bed and
Breakfast, who conceived the idea of a "Christmas in New
Market." Jane's husband Edgar was quite active in planning
New Market Days, but Jane saw the need for a similar event
during the Christmas holidays. She and Isabelle Kindness
co-chaired the first such event in 1979. Jane recalls how
"Everyone took a turn at being in charge for two or three
years at a time." In 2003, members of the New Market

Grange took over this role from Suzie Shenos, who had organized the celebration for several years before that.

My first experience at Christmas in New Market was in December 1989 when I covered the event for the Mt. Airy Courier-Gazette, as it was known then. The celebration was a particularly successful and enjoyable event that year. Hundreds of visitors came to town, walked the streets, and shopped for antiques and handmade craft items as well as other holiday gifts and decorations. Clayton Magee was the organizer that year, and his wife Nancy was responsible for planning all forms of entertainment. Christmas music filled the streets and shops. There were special performances, for example, by the Mt. Airy Full Gospel Church, and several other musical groups and individual entertainers. There were rides in horse-drawn carriages and buggies, a tradition for many years that continues to this day. Santa Claus was there on Main Street, as customary, to delight visiting children. At the New Market Grange, Shirley Burall was very much in charge, proudly claiming that she and her friends had roasted 200 pounds of beef in addition to preparing several soups, country ham, sloppy Joe's, and various pies. "A good time was had by all."   - JFS

Traditionally, this event takes place during the first weekend in December. Homes and shops are specially lighted and decorated much as they were many years ago in New Market. Sometimes, a decorating contest is held to encourage residents and shop-owners to dress up their buildings for the holiday event. Members of the New Market Garden Club traditionally make wreaths, swags, and other holiday decorations and offer them for sale to visitors. Young people from a local church stage a live nativity scene for passersby. Hot cider, food, and the sounds of holiday music help take the chill out of the air. Sometimes, a light snow transforms the town to the beauty of a picture postcard. At other times, such as in 2003, the snow is overly abundant and deters

Candle-making Demonstration By Tamala Ballou at 2003 "Christmas in New Market."

visitors. Snowstorms on two successive days just prior to the weekend of 6-7 December created problems not encountered in recent times. Callers on Saturday morning were advised: "The town is still digging out." Most activities planned for Saturday, 6 December, had to be postponed until that Sunday.

Featured attractions on Sunday included the traditional tree-lighting ceremony and singing of carols in Messanelle Park on Main Street, a visit by Santa Claus at the hospitality center in the Messianic Lodge, and singing by the "Catoctones" barbershop quartet. Also, there is an old-time cooking demonstration in the log building along Strawberry Alley, with its host, Bud Rossig, dressed in traditional garb. Baked goods and craft items were available at the fire hall and also at the Grange. A number of New Market residents attended the event in their period costumes, a very colorful sight. There also was an appearance by the "Moon Sisters" Civil War re-enactors, who once more amused visitors with their mischief.

The numbers of visitors to New Market during recent annual celebrations has decreased compared to those of years past. As mentioned, adverse weather can be an important factor. Traffic and parking are also considerations, and perhaps new methods of promoting these events will be considered. New Market Days and Christmas in New Market have enjoyed a long and popular run, thanks to the planning and hard work of many. There are residents and shop-owners in town who want this tradition to continue. Some are interested because of the business it brings.   Others have expressed more altruistic motives. Long-time resident June Snowden puts it this way:

> *We need to bring the people back to New Market. We have such a beautiful town here. We need to let them know. We need to interest them in coming here.*

Bicentennial Marker in New Market's Messanelle Park on Main Street.

CHAPTER 19

Volunteer Fire Company

New Market maintains its own fire department, right on Main Street, but this was not always the case. The idea to establish a fire department originated at a December 1954 meeting of the local Lions Club. Members were talking about possible projects for the coming year when Dr. Joseph Lerner proposed that they consider starting a fire company to serve the town.

Backrow - Lucian Falconer, John Scheel, Thomas Maker, Austen Main, Bill Clark, Clifford Watkins, Noah King, Robert Windsor, Lloyd Boyer, Jerome Wilcom, Ray Zimmerman, Eugene Zimmerman
Seated - Ralph Brashear, Merhle Wachter, Charles Wood, Frank Smith, Charles Poole, Charles Wilcom, James Hahn

First Fire Company Members, 1955. Photo Courtesy of New Market Fire Company.

Reaction from the community was positive, and members decided to proceed with the proposal. On 15 January 1955, a New Market District meeting took place at the Grange Hall, with Judge Charles Moylan presiding. It was at this meeting that the New Market District Volunteer Fire Company was organized, with the following directors being appointed:

William Browning	Raymond Houston
Charles Cline, Jr.	Charles McA. Jones
Raymond Day	Merhle Murphy
Lucien Falconer, Sr.	Edward Widmayer
Robert Gillett	Charles Wilcom
Charles Gove	

It was the 15th fire company to be organized and established in Frederick County. Incorporated on 24 February 1955, the New Market Fire Company named the following persons to be its first officers:

Clyde Smith, President	Merhle Wachter, Treasurer
John Umberger, First Vice-President	Clifford Watkins, Jr., Secretary
	James R. Hahn, Fire Chief
C.H. Watkins, Sr., Second Vice-President	Leroy Huff, First Assistant Chief
Charles Wood, Financial Secretary	Ralph L. Brashear, Second Assistant Chief

Meetings were held in the old Grange Hall on S. Eighth Alley.

Naturally, the new fire company needed equipment and funds. Together, the firefighters and members of the Lions Club canvassed the community for support and donations. They managed to raise enough money to purchase a new fire engine, which arrived in May 1955. It was a 1955 Ford 500-gallon pumper ordered from the American Fire Apparatus Company of Battle Creek, Michigan. It was called Engine 15 (but later was renamed Engine 151 when the current

Fire Crew of 1959 with New Market's First Fire Truck, a 1955 Ford. Standing are Gene Zimmerman (L) and Bill Clark and Kneeling are (L-R): Bill Wilcom, Ronny Wilcom, Tommy Maher, and Knolton Burgee. Photo Courtesy of Barbara Zimmerman.

Frederick County central alarm was established.) The engine was housed in a garage across from the present firehouse. On 11 June that same year, a Presentation Day celebration took place at the New Market Elementary School on Main Street. Judge Charles E. Moylan was master of ceremonies, and there was an address by Maryland Governor Theodore R. McKeldin. After the formalities, the first of many firehouse dinners to come was served.

During its first year of operation, the New Market Fire Company responded to between fifty and seventy-five fire calls. (For comparison, there were 2,306 such calls in the Year 2003.) Former president Ronald L. "Ronnie" Harshman recalls that residents would call an emergency number in Jim Hahn's home, and Hahn's wife Ruby would

Tommy Maher and Gene Zimmerman Clearing Fire Hoses at the Fire Pond North of Town in 1957. Photo Courtesy of New Market Fire Company.

take the call and then forward the message to all volunteers via a telephone chain.

Important ingredients at any firehouse are recruitment and training of personnel. New Market was generous with its volunteers, and twenty-one of them underwent an exhaustive basic training course from 3 June to 14 October 1955. Fifteen completed the advanced basic course in 1956. In March of that year, the fire company bought the Baker property in New Market, including a house and some five acres of land to be used for a firehouse and carnival grounds. The first carnival held there in July 1956 was considered very successful.

The firefighters erected two buildings on the carnival grounds in 1957, using wood donated by members of the community. Later, the Baker house was demolished, and a new fire hall was built with funds being raised by the firefighters and the Lions Club. The firehouse was built in 1959 almost entirely by members of the fire company, and was modified in 1966.

A Ladies Auxiliary with twenty-five charter members formed on 25 August 1955 to aid the firefighters during fires and to help families whose homes had burned. Ruby Hahn was the Auxiliary's first president, and the organization soon had fifty-one members. The Auxiliary and firefighters also combined their efforts to conduct the first Firemen's Parade and Carnival that same year. Subsequently, the Auxiliary held a variety of fund-raising events, for example, to furnish the new fire hall kitchen. The organization had card parties, rummage and bake sales, and members served at the annual firemen's fall supper. Auxiliary presidents in those early years included Mrs. Hahn, Mrs. Joseph Lerner, Mrs. Ralph Brashear, and Mrs. Allen Kinsey.

Hail to the Chief

Jerry Shanks joined the New Market fire company in 1966. He had been a firefighter in his home state of Ohio before moving to Maryland. He recalls that he had no intention at that time of making firefighting a career. But, after hearing New Market's fire alarm sound time and again, his heart stirred, his blood surged, and he had to become involved once more. Jerry has held a number of offices in the organization but was Fire Chief for some eleven years until stepping down in 1997.

One of the highlights of Jerry's career as Fire Chief was in the early 1990s. The White House called him at midnight and asked him to have an ambulance and crew the following day at Holly Hills Country Club, a mile or so west of New

New Market Crew with Presidential Helicopter. Photo Courtesy of Jerry Shanks.

President Bush Waves Farewell to the Standby Crew of New Market Firefighters. Photo Courtesy of Jerry Shanks.

Market. President George Herbert Walker Bush would be arriving by helicopter to play a round of golf there. Of course, Jerry was there to meet the entourage consisting of not one but three helicopters. "The first helicopter was for the press," he recalls. "The second had some press representatives but was mostly military personnel, and the third carried President Bush." Maryland Governor William Donald Schaefer also was present.

President Bush made the most of a beautiful day in the New Market environs, enjoying a fine game of golf. When he finished and returned to his helicopter, he stopped, turned and asked, "Where is the Chief?" Jerry stepped forward and took the President's outstretched hand and then that of the Governor. "I shook hands with the Governor of Maryland and the President of the United States all in one day," Jerry recalls with some pride.

It was an experience that was to be repeated. President Bush seemed to like golfing at Holly Hills. "We stood by two or three times," Jerry remembers, "then they brought engines out from Fort Detrick (in Frederick)."

Jerry's wife Susan also is a firefighter in New Market – and there is a story Jerry tells about that:

> *Years ago, any white male over the age of 18 could be a volunteer firefighter. Later (with desegregation), it was changed to every male over the age of 18. Then, in the 1970s, when the fire company wanted to buy a Jeep vehicle from the federal government, it had to be changed again to anyone over the age of 18. As a*

Kim Harshman Does the Grilling, with Fellow Firefighters Looking on in Anticipation.

> *result, we got the Jeep, and my wife Susan became a firefighter. Now, years later, we have an old Jeep, and we still have Susan.*

Susan Shanks has been just as committed to the fire service as her husband has over the years. In addition to being a firefighter, she has also been very active in coordinating events sponsored by the fire company.

There have been eight fire chiefs thus far in the fire company's forty-nine years. They were James Hahn, Robert Windsor, Jerry Shanks, William Stem, Vernon Walker, David Yankey, Brian Yankey, and Charles Steed (current chief).

Fatality

Fellow volunteers are still feeling the loss of a fallen comrade, Michael J. Wilcom (34), who succumbed to a heart attack while fighting a fire on 24 May 1993. Wilcom was a Deputy Chief in New Market at the time. Very popular among his peers, Mike is greatly missed by those who knew him.

Ambulance Service

The New Market District Volunteer Fire Company served the local area well for more than two decades since it was established. But, until 1979, ambulance services had to be provided by crews from neighboring cities or towns. Because of growth in the New Market area, the town decided then to take on the responsibility of providing ambulance

Firefighters Cheka Godbey, Dot Clark, Barbara Zimmerman, and Helen Nusbaum. Photo Courtesy of New Market Fire Company.

service there. The fire company purchased a 1979 Wheel Coach on a Ford chassis as its first ambulance and put it into service on the night of 19 December 1979.   Designated "Ambulance 159," it was equipped with the latest medical supplies and rescue tools available at the time. The New Market ambulance responded to the County's Central Alarm, as do the ambulances of other fire companies in Frederick County. In preparation for providing such service, the fire company had trained approximately twenty volunteers in the spring of 1979 as emergency medical technicians. The new ambulance service was dedicated officially at an open house on 13 January 1980, when the twenty-fifth anniversary of the fire company was being celebrated.

Former Fire Chiefs James Hahn and Jerry Shanks. Photo Courtesy of Jerry Shanks.

Currently, the New Market Fire Company has four engines, three ambulances, one tanker, two brush trucks, and a rescue boat.

Preparing for the Future

Efforts are being made, at the time of this writing, to raise money for a new fire hall. For example, in December 2003, two special fund-raisers included a craft and gift show and a "Country Breakfast With Santa" at the firehouse. The weekly Friday-night bingo is another traditional source of revenue. Actual construction of a new fire hall, however, must await the introduction of public water service to the town from Frederick County.

The New Market District Volunteer Fire and Rescue Company, as it is now known, will be fifty years old in 2005.

New Market District
Fire and Rescue Company Presidents

Clyde Smith, 1955-1957
William Browning, 1958-1959
Wm. Franklin Smith, 1960-1963
Ralph Brashear, 1964-1965
William Earl Ridgely, 1966
Charles Cline, 1967-1970
James Hahn (Honorary) 1971
Charles Cline, 1972-1975
Ethan "Pete" Summers, 1976
John McThenia, 1977-1980
Robert Weller, 1981-1993
Ronald Harshman, 1994-1995
Pat Staley, 1996-1997
Joanie Wachter, 1998-1999
Rick Gue, 2000
Maurice Hayter, 2001-2002
Shirley King, 2003-

911 Memorial Project

New Market's firefighters were deeply saddened by the tragic events of September 11, 2001 when hijacked airliners struck the World Trade Center's Twin Towers in New York, the Defense Department's Pentagon Building in Virginia, and a crash field in Pennsylvania. The 347 firefighters who died as the result of these acts of terrorism were comrades to all in their chosen profession. Shirley King, current president of the New Market Volunteer Fire and Rescue Company, and her fellow firefighters determined that they would like to do something to ensure that those who had fallen in this attack would not be forgotten.

The specific proposal to build a Twin Towers memorial at the New Market fire station, however, came from an outsider, Leo McHale of Walkersville, Maryland. Leo tells how he was recovering from heart surgery after the "911" attacks when he met some of the burn victims rescued from the badly damaged Pentagon. It was a life-altering experience for McHale, redirecting his attention from his own circumstances to the creation of a memorial dedicated to the men and women who served so unselfishly in their proud profession.

Leo says that he chose New Market for this memorial because of its central location within three hours of New York, the crash location in Pennsylvania, and the Pentagon site in Virginia. He approached Shirley with his idea to design such a memorial, and she agreed. They would link the effort to fundraising for the new fire hall.

A groundbreaking ceremony took place, very appropriately, on September 11, 2004. Components of the planned memorial designed by McHale have evolved to the point where they now include:

- "The 911 Walk,"[®] comprised of 1,000-plus bricks commemorating the number of lives lost and bearing the motto, "Walk in My Steps;"
- "The 911 Wall,"[®] commemorating the 2,998 victims at the Twin Towers;
- "The 911 Twin Towers,"[®] each 9 feet 11 inches tall and the base will be 9 feet by 11 feet by 1 foot (signifying the date 9-11-01) with 347 bricks representing the number of firefighters who died as a result of the attack on the Twin Towers; and
- "The 911 Memorial,"[®] the icon universally associated with this national tragedy, is McHale's creation based on the United States Postal Stamp introduced on June 7, 2002.[57]

The site of these memorials will be behind the old fire hall in New Market just in front of the planned new fire hall, which will also house a planned 911 museum.

In recognition of his hard work and devotion to this ambitious memorial project, the New Market Volunteer Fire and Rescue Company recently made Leo McHale an "Honorary Firefighter."

---

[57] Mr. Leo F. McHale has graciously granted permission for these copyrighted titles, to which he owns the rights, to be used in this book.

Design for New Market 911 Memorial, Courtesy of Leo McHale.

CHAPTER 20

The Hahn Company

Big Company, Big Trucks, in a Very Small Town

The Hahn Transportation Company at 90 West Main Street dates to 1933 when James R. Hahn gave up farming and entered the trucking business. He first took over his father's milk route, hauling milk from dairy farms in the area with his 1930 Ford truck. He also delivered grain and other farm produce to local dairies as well as feed mills and canneries in the general area. Soon thereafter, he purchased a house and land, for $5,500 in New Market, where the business remains.

Hahn began operating from New Market in 1934 and several years later added ten trucks to his fleet. One of the early tasks involved hauling large quantities of lime, for example, to tobacco farmers in the eastern shore area of Maryland. Jim Hahn built his family-owned business into a twenty-four-hour hauling service, operating seven days a week.

It may be more than coincidence that the New Market fire hall is located next to the Hahn Company. As already indicated, Hahn was named New Market's first fire chief in 1955. Former Fire Chief Jerry Shanks worked for the Hahn Company from 1974 to 2001, and there have been many others who combined their careers at Hahn with their volunteer service at the fire company.

Founder James Hahn worked thirty-seven years before retiring. His daughter Rebecca and her husband Robert Windsor took over the helm in 1972. He became President of Hahn Transportation, and she assumed the positions of Chairman of the Board and Chief Executive Officer. They both retired in 2001. Their daughter, Barbara J. Windsor, currently is President and Chief Operations Officer. The family business has grown over almost seventy years to the point where they now have more than 200 employees. And yet, they continue to emphasize "family values and family service."

While Hahn's headquarters remains in New Market, a similar trucking company in Dayton, Virginia, was acquired in 1972. This acquisition resulted in a greatly expanded customer area serviced by four regional terminals in Maryland and Virginia. From the days when Jim Hahn started trucking with one two-axle Ford truck, the family business has grown to the point where it now boasts more than 500 licensed pieces of equipment. The expanded business includes flatbed trailers for carrying bags of dry products or blocks of aluminum; dump trailers for deliveries of sand, gravel, and aggregates; and insulated trailers for transporting food-grade products. Hahn also offers specialized trailers for transporting petroleum products as well as limestone and concrete products. Periodic maintenance services take place at regional sites in Dayton and Front Royal, Virginia, as well as in New Market and Union Bridge, Maryland.

The original house bought by Hahn was demolished in 1987. To replace it, the Windsors put up a building in the Federal style so as to blend in with the historic homes of New Market.

CHAPTER 21

Outlook for the Future

Changes In Zoning

"New Market's main problem is that residents don't have a butcher, baker, or candlestick-maker. They have to go elsewhere for services." This is how one New Market resident and shop-owner put it, adding that local zoning laws "are archaic and over-intrusive and invasive." Others disagree.

Zoning restrictions traditionally have been very conservative and were designed both to preserve the historic nature of the town and to enhance its reputation as a center for antique shopping. Uses other than antique businesses have had to be considered on an individual basis as exceptions to the approved use.

The New Market Town Council considered a proposal in 2003 to expand the types of businesses permitted within the town limits to include, for example: a bakery, ice cream parlor, professional offices, flower shop, pottery/jewelry stores, art galleries, and so forth. Those in favor of the proposal argued that the town would benefit from allowing a bit more diversity in shops and services, perhaps making it more attractive to tourists and businesses alike. Others expressed their concerns that the town's long-held reputation as a center for antiquing might suffer from allowing more flexible zoning. On 14 April 2004, the town council finally settled this issue by deciding, on a three to one vote with one member absent, to allow other types of businesses in New Market. This new policy went into effect the following day, but its full ramifications may not be known for some time.

By July 2004, the first of these newly allowed non-antique shops, "The Little Pottery Shop," had arrived in the historic district of New Market, at 75B W. Main Street. For a long while, its owner, Tameria "Tammy" Martinez, hoped to locate her small business there "to get closer to the retail traffic." She said, "New Market looked perfect for what we have," referring to her line of hand-made pottery. But, under the old zoning ordinance, the district had been almost exclusively for antiques, as indicated above. When that policy changed, Tammy decided to take another look and then quickly made her move. She hopes that other business people may take a look too.

Ms. Martinez makes most of the pottery that she sells but also represents crafters from Ijamsville and Walkersville and plans to be adding the works of others with a variety of designs. People come to see working artisans, and they come to buy. Tammy says that, when she moved her business to New Market, she brought her client base as well. She predicts, "Others will too."

Addressing Traffic Problems

When interviewed in December 2002, former Mayor Rick Fleshman stated that the number one problem in New Market is the traffic through town. "Six thousand cars go through town every day," he said, adding:

It is a state road, so any changes have to be approved by the state. The state would like to turn the road over to the town, but the town would have to maintain the road, do its own snow plowing, and so forth. It would be too expensive.

The reason for the greatly increased flow of traffic through New Market in recent years is that great numbers of people have bought homes in nearby housing developments to the north and west, such as Lake Linganore at Eaglehead and Spring Ridge. After working elsewhere, many return to their homes by way of Interstate 70. Exiting at Route 75, they then have to drive through New Market to one of the few north-south routes, such as Boyer's Mill Road, Yeagertown Road, or Eaglehead Drive – all of which become seriously overloaded at such times. An alternate route is badly needed. According to Fleshman, various proposals were being considered to change the county's Comprehensive Plan. One idea involves the improvement of Crickenberger Road linking Route 75 north of New Market with Lake Linganore at Eaglehead. This project might reduce the flow of traffic through New Market and along Boyers Mill Road. Other alternatives are being explored as well.

For the most part, the citizens of New Market would prefer to have it remain a small town just as it has been for more than two centuries. On the other hand, the only solution to the problem of heavy and increasing traffic down Main Street seems to be the annexation of nearby lands to the north of town through which a bypass road, such as the Crickenberger bypass, could be constructed. In February 2004, New Market Mayor Winslow Burhans asked the Frederick County Planning Commission to support such a bypass in order to relieve the serious traffic problem on Main Street. In this regard, he cited 2002 State Highway Administration figures showing that more than 8,000 vehicles drive through New Market on a daily basis.

In June of 2004, Mayor Burhans put daily traffic flow in New Market at 8,300 vehicles and reported estimates of 10,000 by 2005 and 16,000 vehicles per day sometime in the next ten years. A resolution of this intensifying problem will have to be found soon.

Other Problems

Burhans pointed out that New Market and other small municipalities in Frederick County face additional problems related to growth, such as relieving overcrowding in the schools (especially needed at the high school level) upgrading water services, and adding recreational facilities. To accomplish what should be done, he seeks a greater partnership between the county and the municipalities. In particular, he sees the need to prioritize, control, and manage growth. Pointing to the joint effort he envisions being needed by the county and the towns, Mayor Burhans suggests that the townspeople must consider whether they want a "Treaty of Versailles" or a "Marshall Plan." In other words, as he says, "Is the town going to get involved?"

One specific approach being taken by the mayor with some success is to seek developer-funded support, for example, to expand the schools.

Like his predecessors, Mayor Burhans takes very seriously his responsibility to help preserve the historic nature of his town, emphasizing that its history greatly predates the period of its prominence as an antique center. He emphasizes the responsibility of local citizens, as well, to maintain their historic homes inside and out, however expensive that might be. He regards the structural integrity of the buildings to be far more important than, for example, the color of its siding or shingles.

Future Annexations

In the late 1970s, a local builder, Mike Sponseller, succeeded in building a development of seventy-five small homes just west of the town limits at the time. The Town of New Market annexed this development in 1979, and home construction there proceeded into the 1980s. It was a significant first step in the growth of this historic place. Additional annexations thus became a possibility.

The November 2003 Staff Draft of the New Market Region Plan, by the Frederick County Division of Planning, presented three residential growth scenarios for the Town of New Market. If any, or all, of these scenarios were to come to pass, the town's population could increase greatly, and the character of the town could be seriously affected.

When this draft plan was presented, there already were two proposed developments (Royal Oaks and Brinkley Manor) under review for annexation. Growth Scenario 1 alone would add these additional subdivisions: New Market West, New Market Farms, The Meadows at New Market, Woodspring, Glenn at Woodspring, and certain surrounding parcels. All of these developments are relatively close to the historic town. Growth Scenarios 2 and 3 comprise additional areas for future development and consideration for annexation by the Town of New Market. These areas, however, lie farther to the north of town and close to the Lake Linganore and West Winds developments.

"We are likely to get another annexation request, for the Casey-Blentlinger Property," Mayor Burhans advises. Developer D. R. Horton has a contract to build some 2,100 units there, according to Burhans.

In proposing areas to be annexed, Mayor Burhans recently cited the necessity to solve the town's traffic problems. He explains his rationale for these annexations as follows:

> *In conclusion, the Town of New Market only proposes to annex those properties that contribute to the public good or increase our tax base. In order to show good faith towards mitigating the effects upon public facilities, we have left out properties that although contiguous to the Town do not aid to solving traffic or other problems. It is our intention to be a financially self-sufficient good neighbor to all in the New Market region.*

What Lies Ahead

From origins as a farm community and stopover point for weary travelers in the late eighteenth century and throughout the 1800's, to becoming the "Antiques Capital of Maryland"® during the twentieth century, the small, but special Town of New Market, Maryland, has survived and made its mark in history. Much of its success can be attributed to great leaders such as its founders, Nicholas Hall and William Plummer, entrepreneurs Samuel and Silas Utz, and Stoll Kemp; as well as long-time Mayors Franklin Smith and Franklin Shaw.

Messanelle Park in the Town of New Market.

 In the beginning, German Quakers and people of English, Irish, and Scottish heritage came to live together and formed a town. For some, it meant overcoming the scourge of slavery and surviving in the very midst of a great civil war. On the very heels of the Great Depression, they turned to relics of the past – antiques – as a means of support and commerce. Through it all, these people valued and maintained their historic homes for others to see and appreciate, even as they still do today.

Change will come to New Market. Housing developments already are beginning to surround the town. As annexations are approved, they will greatly inflate the long-static population there. Increased population means more local voters being registered, more demands for services, and, no doubt, new ideas for the future of this venerable place.

At the front of this book, we noted that the town was described in 1886 in this fashion:

> _Blessed with pure water, good hygiene, pure air, and good crops, it is a pleasant place to live._

No matter what changes lie in store, New Market, hopefully, will continue to be as special and pleasant a place to live as it was "**Back When ...**"

Selected Bibliography

Atlas of Frederick County Maryland, C.O. Titus & Co., Philadelphia, Pa., 1873.

Barnes, Robert (compiler), *Maryland Marriages, 1778-1800,* Genealogical Publishing Co., Inc., Baltimore, 1979.

Bowie, Effie Gwynn, *Across the Years in Prince Georges County,* Genealogical Publishing, Baltimore, 1975 Reprint of 1947 ed.

Brittanica Micropoedia, 15th ed., Vol. 3, 2003.

Cooling, B. Franklin, *Monocacy: The Battle that Saved Washington,* White Mane Publishing Co., Inc., Beidel Printing House, Inc., Shippensburg, Pa., 1997.

Frederick County, Maryland, *Official Poll of Presidential Election, 1796.*

Frederick County, *Comprehensive Master Plan, New Market, Maryland,* Frederick County Planning Commission, 1969.

Frederick County, *New Market Region Plan,* Frederick County Division of Planning, Dept. of Planning and Zoning, (Staff Draft), 2003.

Goldsborough, C.E. Writer, *New Market,* 1936.

Grigsby, S. Earl, and Harold Hoffsomer, *Rural Social Organization in Frederick County, Maryland,* Univ. of Md. (College Park, Md.) Department of Sociology and Agricultural Experiment Station, March *1949.*

Hattery, Thomas H., *Western Maryland – A Profile,* Lomond Books, Mt. Airy, Md., 1980.

Hopkins, H. Hanford 4th, *Captain John Hopkins, Mariner of Philadelphia, and Bideford, in Devon, and His Alleged Forebears and Descendants,* a narrative, Baltimore, 1977.

Jourdan, Elise Greenup, *Early Families of Southern Maryland,* Family Line Publications, Westminster, Md., 1993.

Lewis, J. Frank, *The Maryland Directory,* Baltimore, 1882.

Manakee, Harold R., *Maryland In the Civil War, Maryland Historical Society*, Baltimore, 1969 Reprint of 1961 ed.

Marck, John T., *The Seventh State – A History,* Creative Impressions, Glen Arm, Md., c1995.

Martin, John Stanwood, *Genealogical Index to Frederick County, Maryland,* Vol. III, Conlin's Copy Center, Malvern, Pa., 1992.

Maryland: A History, 1632-1974, Maryland Historical Society, Baltimore, 1974.

Myers, Margaret E., *Marriage Licenses of Frederick County, Md., 1778-1810,* Family Line Publications, Silver Spring, Md., 1986.

Newman, Harry Wright, *Lineage of Robert Plummer and Anne Arundel Gentry,* Vol. II, Family Line Publications, Washington, D.C., 1990.

Peden, Henry C., Jr., *Quaker Records of Northern Maryland, Births, Deaths, Marriages, and Abstracts from the Minutes of Monthly Meetings, 1716-1800,* Family Line Publications, Westminster, Md., 1993.

Peden, *Revolutionary Patriots of Frederick County, Maryland, 1775 - 1783,* Family Line Publications, Westminster, Md., 1995.

Raitz, Karl (editor), *The National Road,* Johns Hopkins Univ. Press, Baltimore & London, 1996.

Rhodes, Robert Hunt, *All for the Union, The Civil War Diary and Letters of Elisha Hunt Rhodes,* Orion Books, 2nd ed., New York, 1991.

Rollo, Vera Foster, *Your Maryland – A History, 1632-1974,* Maryland Historical Press, Lanham, Md., 3rd revised ed., 1976, and 5th revised ed., 1993.

Russell, Donna Valley, *Frederick County Maryland Wills, 1744-1794,* Catoctin Press, New Market, Md., 2002.

Scharf J. Thomas, *History of Western Maryland,* Regional Publishing Co., Baltimore, Vols. I, II, & III and Index to Vol. I, 1968 Reprint of 1882 Ed.

Shaw, James R. and Carl Larsen, Janet Davis, *Historic Site Survey, New Market Region,* Frederick County, 1994, revised in 1996.

Smith, Herbert F., *The Plummer Ancestry of Herbert F. Smith, indexed and produced by Robert S. Smith,* Silver Spring, Md., 1995.

Toomey, Daniel Carroll, *The Civil War in Maryland,* Toomey Press, Baltimore, 1993.

Tracey, Grace L. and John P. Derr, *Pioneers of Old Monocacy: The Early Settlement of Frederick County, Maryland,* Genealogical Publishing Co., Inc., Baltimore, 1987.

Williams, T.J.C. and Folger McKinsey, Vol. I., Reprint of 1910 ed., Regional Publishing Co., Baltimore, 1967 and 1979.

World Book, Volumes 4, 19, and 21, Chicago, 2001.

World Book, Volume 1, Chicago, 2002.

Wright, F. Edward, *Anne Arundel County Church Records of the 17th and 18th Centuries,* Family Line Publications, Westminster, Md., n.d.

Research was conducted at the Maryland Room of the C. Burr Artz Library, the Historical Society of Frederick County, and the Register of Wills at the Frederick County Courthouse, all in the City of Frederick, Maryland - with additional information acquired through an intensive series of personal interviews in the Town of New Market and its environs.

Personal Interviews

New Market:
Rev. Mary-Patricia Ashby, 3-2-04
Glenn Berkhousen, 11-24-03
Winslow Burhans III, 6-18-04
Karen Carrier, 12-13-02
Dora Connolly, 10-24-02
Leonard Curry, 9-29-02
Lucien Falconer, Jr., 3-19-04 and
    4-5-04
Rick Fleshman, 12-14-02
Ronald Harshman, 2-2-04
Bill Hartman, 2-5-03
Jim Higgs, 10-9-02
Shirley King, 2-4-04
John Lancey, 6-3-04
Mark Lawson, 7-5-04 (approx.
    date)
Tommy Maher, Sr., 3-23-04
Tameria Martinez, 7-29-04
McHale, Leo F., 12-1-04
Ruth and Betty Metz (by phone),
    8-4-04
Patricia Morrow, 12-2-02
Rita Mueller, 2-5-03, 6-4-04, 11-
    30-04
Sharon Press, 6-25-03
Susan Proakis, 7-18-03
Doug and Pat Racine, 2-8-03
Gene Rooney, 1-31-04
Edgar W. Rossig III, 9-3-02*
Jane Rossig, 11-20-02
Jose Salaverri, 6-9-04
Howard Selby, 6-23-04
Jerry and Susan Shanks, 1-23 &
    28-04
Shirley Shaw, 11-13-02

Colleen Shook, 3-1-04
Wm. Franklin Smith, 11-25-02
June Snowden, 3-11&16-04
Ken Valentino, 6-15-04
Julie Vogl, 7-18-03
Sue Wilson, 9-27-02, 6-11-04
Rebecca Windsor (via mail), 5-28-
    04
Carla Wolf, 1-29-04
Nick Wood, 10-21-02 & 5-28-04
Barbara Zimmerman, 3-11-04
Paul Zimmerman, 6-25-04

Catonsville:
Charlotte Houser, 4-5-04

Frederick:
Ida Lu Brown, 4-30-04
Mary Anna Burgee (by phone), 8-
    4-04
G. Monroe Free (by phone), 2003

Ijamsville:
Marguerite Burgee, 8-2-04

Monrovia:
George Helta, 2-12-04 & 4-17-04
Betty Jeffers, 4-21-04 & 5-1-04

Mt. Airy:
Jean Brinkley, 8-18-03

(*) This was the first of a series of
many sessions over a two-year
period.

About the Author

Joseph F. Seng is a graduate of the University of Nebraska at Omaha and the National War College in Washington, D.C. As an officer in the United States Air Force, he served on a combat crew aboard a B-29 Bomber during the Korean War. After more than four years in the military, he took up a 29-year government career in intelligence. During most of this period, he and his wife, Joyce, lived in Rockville, Maryland, where they raised their five children.

After he retired from government, Joe and Joyce moved to Frederick County, Maryland, and he began a career as a writer and author. He wrote full-page, human-interest, stories each week for a local newspaper for several years. He also conducted genealogical research of his own family and that of his wife, going back almost 200 years. This work culminated in the publication of a hardback book entitled "Our Family History" in 1997. This was followed in 2002 by "Land of Promise: A Brief History of Monrovia, Maryland."

Why this book about New Market? Mr. Seng explains:

> *I like history, I like to meet people and hear the stories they have to tell, and I like to write. Living but a few miles from New Market over the past seventeen years, my wife and I have made many friends there, and I wanted to discover and preserve the history of their very special town.*

Photo Courtesy of PCA International, Inc.